DATE DUE

SUITABLE FOR CHILDREN?

Controversies in Children's Literature

Suitable for Children?

CONTROVERSIES IN CHILDREN'S LITERATURE

Edited and Introduced

by

NICHOLAS TUCKER

UNIVERSITY OF CALIFORNIA PRESS

Berkeley and Los Angeles

First published 1976
Second impression 1978

UNIVERSITY OF CALIFORNIA PRESS
Berkeley and Los Angeles, California

ISBN: 0–520–03236–5
Library of Congress Catalog Card Number: 76–6016

Introduction, Notes and Selection
© Nicholas Tucker 1976

Printed in Great Britain

Dedicated to my sister, Elisabeth
and to my brothers
Martin, Patrick and Andrew,
who have also always
enjoyed children's books and comics.

CONTENTS

Contents

ACKNOWLEDGEMENTS

The Editor and Publishers are grateful to the following for permission to reproduce copyright material: Miss D.E. Collins for 'The Fear of the Film' by G.K. Chesterton. *Books for Your Children* for 'Bits strewn all over the Page' by Elizabeth Gard. *New Society* for 'Once More into the Mangle' by Angela Carter, 'What do Children learn from War Comics?' by Nicholas Johnson, 'Miss Potter and the Little Rubbish' and 'Teach your Baby to Rule' by Patrick Richardson, 'Flight of the Imagination' by Mary Warnock and 'Tolkien's Fictions' by Michael Wood. *New Statesman* for 'The Real Cleanup' by J.B. Priestley. Oxford University Press for the extract from *The Oxford Book of Stories for Juniors* (Teachers' Book) by James Britton. *The Junior Bookshelf* for 'The Educational and Moral Values of Folk and Fairy Tales' by J. Langfeldt. The *Sunday Times* for 'Things that go bump in the Night' by Catherine Storr. *The Times Literary Supplement* for 'Oh! Please Mr. Tiger' by Janet Hill, 'Anti-Superman' and 'The Children's Falstaff' by Nicholas Tucker, and 'The Rainbow Surface' by Jill Paton Walsh. *Where,* (Advisory Centre for Education) for 'Why Folk Tales and Fairy Stories live Forever' by Catherine Storr, and 'Comics Today' by Nicholas Tucker.

PREFACE

Many adults must feel that they are, to some extent, 'mini-experts' on children's literature, simply because of the almost unavoidable contact with books and comics we have when young. In this way, children's literature, unlike some other topics, is fortunate: it can usually depend upon an initially interested response. But this sort of popular expertise has its limitations: new writers will have sprouted, others withered, during the interval of growing up, and generalisations based on such memories may arise from narrow experience and confused recollection at that. Everyone has a right to his own nostalgia, of course, and memories of children's books may quite naturally be as pleasantly self-indulgent as any other childhood recall. But this sort of whimsy is perhaps less excusable in the views of some educators or book reviewers who really should know better.

In this present volume, therefore, I have put together what I hope is a useful collection of writing by various authors and critics on some aspects of children's literature. This is in no sense a comprehensive introduction; rather, I have chosen essays and reviews, often not easily accessible elsewhere, that group themselves into five related, and sometimes controversial topics. As this is an area that has often attracted more than its fair share of cosy, ineffectual criticism in the past, I have preferred to choose from sharper critics who are concerned with wider issues which are often more stimulating. Although most of my selection has been from the 20th century, I have also chosen some earlier writing that still seems relevant to some of the arguments heard today.

But is the whole subject worth much attention, beyond raising a few affectionate memories of childhood itself? I

11

would certainly have hoped so: there are some very good children's books, both ancient and modern, which deserve notice from child and adult. If potentially bookish children never get near such works, and if the adults around them persist in out of date, patronising attitudes towards children's literature, this may result in a lost opportunity that I, for one, would regret. No one has ever managed to measure what it is that the right book can give to the reader at the right time, but there is probably enough agreement to say that something good *can* happen. To miss this chance when the reader is ready for it may be a sad waste of potential on both sides. How serious such a waste might be is impossible to say; it could simply mean the child misses a certain type of privacy and fun. On the other hand, many autobiographies have described the delights and excitements of reading when young, sometimes for children normally denied literature but who, once coming across it, remain hooked for life.

We can never tell which children will react in which way; for some, literature may almost always be something of a bore. It would be unjustifiable to maintain that there is anything necessarily *wrong* with individuals who feel this, whether as children or adults. But given that, every child should at least be offered the opportunity to discover whether he is going to enjoy literature or not. By far the best way to recommend a book is from personal experience of the interest, excitement or whatever else one is then trying to bring to other readers. As I have already said, this sort of interest cannot be drawn exclusively from past childhood experience, yet keeping up with contemporary children's literature may present problems to some adult readers: it is, almost by definition, a field one grows away from. To find one's way back to it later on may imply a certain faith and even suspension of a sense of ridicule: can an adult really afford to be caught reading a children's book for his own enjoyment?

I believe that he can, once he realises the scope and indeed sophistication of some children's literature. In the following pages, therefore, I have tried to bring together aspects of

12

children's literature that might help towards a wider, more stimulating appreciation of the whole topic. Inevitably some subjective feeling for the particular charm of certain children's books still remains, along with what I hope is more rigorous analysis elsewhere, but I would defend this. There can never be a completely objective, depersonalised account of a subject such as this, where the individual needs of both author and reader may inter-act in such differing ways. Rather, I have tried to put together articles that will stimulate readers, whether they be parents with a renewed interest in children's books because of their own growing families, teachers who see the potential in the subject but want to tackle it in a more informed way, or the student or general reader with an interest in this fascinating subject simply in its own right — perhaps the best type of interest of all. For this reason, there are no articles here on *how* to teach children's literature. I am more concerned here with the intrinsic interest of the subject as such; teaching techniques must belong to another book.

Many people have contributed to my own re-discovery of children's books, but I would particularly like to acknowledge Nina Bawden and Edward Blishen as authors, critics and friends, the source of many delightful conversations about this topic in the past and many more, I hope, to come. I would also like to thank Eileen Hall for her hard work preparing the manuscript, Laura Propper for her editorial help, which was invaluable, and my wife for toiling through the proofs with me.

INTRODUCTION

Children's literature has been going strong for about a hundred years; books about this phenomenon are also becoming common, but rather more recently. Another discussion of the same subject needs justification, so perhaps I should state what this book is *not* going to be, taking warning from some of the less successful writing on the subject published recently, and not attempting to duplicate the few really satisfactory studies now available.

For example, I shall not provide a lightning, package-tour around famous contemporary names in children's literature, scattering biographical details, lists of publications and instant critical summaries as we go. The only sound way to appreciate any writer is to read his works; if an introduction is still required, I would recommend John Rowe Townsend's *A Sense of Story*: a thoughtful and well-written critique of nineteen modern children's writers, by an author who is himself a critic and writer for children.

Secondly, I shall not be putting forward any equally hasty historical survey, starting with that first children's bookshop of John Newbery in 1744 (although if authors of this particular type of book have done their homework correctly — not always the case — they will note that Newbery was preceded as a publisher first catering for children in any reasonable scale by Thomas Boreman, who produced some nice little books for juvenile subscribers in 1742). The best such historical survey is Harvey Darton's *Children's Books in England*, although, for a briefer introduction, I would again recommend John Rowe Townsend's *Written for Children*. Otherwise, this particular genre tends to be disappointing, made up of too

15

many breathless plot summaries set in an unconvincing gallop through English social history. Once again, any sort of critical assessment at this pace tends to consist of little more than a few hurried pats on the head.

Lastly, since it is children that are involved, there have been numbers of books that discuss literature for this age group chiefly with regard to its educational value, and this I shall most certainly not attempt to do. At best, this sort of writing can provide the odd, useful title and warn against out-dated methods, such as reading around the class – still alive, along with other educational dinosaurs, in those schools that stand out against modern methods, or perhaps don't even know that such things now exist. At its worst, however, the educational approach to children's literature can be like drowning in the warm milk of human kindness. Metaphors abound: children are compared to growing flowers, opening buds, or tender shoots; the author takes them by the hand (mixing metaphors is quite fair game too), leading them over mountains into the warm, fertile valleys below. Literature it-self shines like a beacon, a searchlight, a sun. But what if some children, unaccountably, don't seem to care for all this bounty? Then, no stone must be left unturned, even if it seems to be providing a little shade for the odd pupil in all this literary heat. He must be wheedled, tricked or loved into literature; after all, every day that goes by is one more possible masterpiece missed. And if he is not reading now, how much more likely is he to join one day that benighted adult army that never reads a novel at all? Try, therefore, to find books from the reader's social background; if these don't work, try books from an opposite social background. It may be that he is looking for variety, and one theory is as good as another in a crisis. If you are reading out books aloud, stop at the most exciting places, to tempt the reluctant reader to go on for himself. If he is undergoing stress in his personal life, such as learning to cope with a new baby or going into hospital for a minor operation, find novels that touch on such things – several book-lists exist for this purpose already, a phenomenon sometimes referred to as 'bibliotherapy'.*

Now the educational case for children's books has of course been argued more subtly than this, and I have listed some of the better books in all these genres in the general bibliography. But I also believe that too much insistence on children's literature as a type of spiritual tonic for the young may lead to a downgrading of its status as literature, in some cases for all ages. One should not have to defend literature on the grounds that it is necessarily good for you; a book is something that exists primarily to provide the reader with a literary experience, something he cannot get elsewhere from other means.

Perhaps my chief objection to so many of the books adopting any of the approaches so far described is the impression too often conveyed of a cosy general view of children's literature. Only something excessively tame could be taken for such an easy ride, and children's literature in fact abounds in contradictions, ambiguities and arguments, making it a fascinating but necessarily complex field for study. Approaches that rely chiefly upon adult nostalgia and educational do-goodism belie the material at our disposal. This is why in the essays collected together here I have preferred writing that brings out some of these controversies, even though I may not always agree with the particular point of view taken. At the same time, I have tried to include other pieces that hint at the richness of much children's literature, easy to over-look from an adult viewpoint that may often relegate it to the general level of other childish activities, like playing hopscotch, reading comics or firing off catapults – all good fun at the time, but perhaps better forgotten when one has really grown up.

An important point to start with, therefore, is the whole question of children's books as literature, sometimes of interest to all readers, even those adults not necessarily

* For example: Hazel Bell, *Situation Books for Under-sixes: A Guide to Books for Reading to Children when Mummy has another Baby, the Child is Going to Hospital and so on* (Kenneth Mason Ltd, 1970).

concerned with education or with reading to their own children. This issue is central to all controversies about the significance or effect of such literature. To put it crudely, are we talking about an art or about mere marketing for children; a field of publishing properly adjustable to the whims of its audience or those who supply it, such as teachers or librarians? There are obviously plenty of books that do fall into this category — those that accompany reading schemes, for example. But to see all children's books in this way would be to make any discussion patronising and diminishing — as so often happens with this subject and concerned primarily with getting the best fit between mass client and producer, as if one were instructing an architect on the shape of a new school swimming pool. Yet if we see the best children's books as literature within its own right, then some of the traditional defences of all creative literature become relevant, where the artist can claim responsibility primarily to himself and his own vision. To believe otherwise would be to under-value both an interesting branch of literature today and the ultimate experience some children can have with books. Or in other words, if we think a certain book important for children, it could be that it is important for the rest of us too, unless we don't think very much of children's taste and perception in the first place. This is not to say that every book for children is of interest for adults; much writing for this age is satisfying to the extent that it simply echoes the immaturity of its audience — the sort of book that children grow out of, and with little to tempt them back. Other books may be much more interesting to everyone; what sort of experience these offer, and where they stand in relation to adult needs and perceptions, is worth further discussion.

In contrast to some others who have written on this question, I do believe that there are intrinsic differences between the best books aimed at children and those written for adults, and that no children's literature could ever be a work of art in the same league as, say, Tolstoy, George Eliot or Dickens. If a writer is aiming at a young audience, he must of necessity restrict himself in certain areas of experience and vocabulary. To be more specific: although children may be highly interested in sex, adult relationships and the pattern – or lack of it – in life itself, there are ways of treating all these subjects that will mean more to an adult than to a child, because of his greater experience of such things. A young reader may get a glimpse of adult life in certain books, and just for these insights a bookish child may be eager to start on books which are in many other ways out of his depth. This does not matter; he can simply re-read them all at a later stage and discover those layers missed the first time through. Of course, this is a common experience at all ages with complex works of art: no single reading will ever reveal everything. But the gap in total comprehension between child and adult understanding is necessarily greater in certain areas which is one reason why children's authors may have to limit themselves, when writing for children, in several important ways.

This is not simply a matter of experience and subject-matter; children also find some literary styles and approaches hard to understand. This generalisation naturally does not work for all children but, on the whole, it is probably true that irony in writing, for example, commonly confuses younger children, used as they are to looking on rather than beneath the surface of things. A reading comprehension test conducted at a teachers' training college revealed that even at this level it was relatively common for students to misunderstand an author's intention, particularly when it came to detecting irony in a literary extract.* In this context, a book like *Candide* may seem to a young reader a rather puzzling, amoral story – to see it as satire may need more detachment and worldly wisdom. Again, children are not commonly good psychologists, tending again to judge behaviour by its surface appearance rather than by any deeper motivation. One of the exciting things books can start doing for children is to introduce them to more complex ways of

* See Pat D'Arcy, *Reading for Meaning,* pp. 182-3 (Hutchinson, 1973).

thinking about people, but this cannot be taken too far too quickly. To get at all near some of the mysteries of human behaviour, most readers will require a wider range of experience and insight than one can commonly hope to find in children, or which one would expect to come across in a children's book.

To take one more point: children when young tend to see the universe as an essentially moral construction, imbued with a sense of 'inherent justice', so that somehow, in the long run, good will always be rewarded and evil eventually punished. Many of them will grow more sceptical over the years, but it still may take some time before a child is emotionally ready to face up to the possibility of an impersonal universe and a casual human existence, whether he is eventually to believe in such a thing or not. Perhaps for this reason, most children's books will end on some note of hope or resolution, whatever the tribulations that may have happened before. This is nothing to do with moralising as such: rather, I think, a feeling for what a younger audience is ready for. A less didactic type of ending might appear meaningless by default, rather than intention, and the author consequently criticised for leaving his audience in the air, rather than on the solid, essentially moralistic ground a child prefers to stand on. G.K. Chesterton once described this 'Day of Judgment' type of dénouement as necessary for all good stories aimed at the young: "For children are innocent and love justice; while most of us are wicked and naturally prefer mercy".

The author writing for adults does not have to accept any of these restrictions, and in this sense is free to draw on all the experience, expression and philosophy at his command. A children's author, I would argue, has ruled himself out from some of these resources. But to say therefore that a book aimed principally at children can never be great literature is not to dismiss it from any other sort of literary consideration. After all, many literary genres aimed at adults deliberately cut down on the range of experience and expression possible. A writer of thrillers may choose to concentrate on plot and action to the extent of neglecting the characters in his story. In this sense, I would suggest that the best children's books fall into another type of literary genre, accessible both to adults and children, and particularly strong in some of the following respects.

For example, when adults write for children, they may also be writing for that part of themselves unfulfilled by the adult culture in which they live. Many of the best children's stories have been drawn out of adults by the active presence of a child audience, so that the original work has something of the character of thinking aloud, or a type of free-association. The results can be entertaining, and also liberating, in that they may reach less accessible parts of an adult imagination – not necessarily hidden childish aspects, but those thoughts and feelings that do not fit easily into a particular adult life style. Lewis Carroll's *Alice* books are obviously candidates here: a contrast to prevalent Victorian thought and writing, and in many ways a commentary on the author himself. What the appeal of these marvellous books might be for the rest of us, it is impossible to say, though many have tried – Martin Gardner's extensive notes in *The Annotated Alice** reveal a graveyard of interpretations, particularly of the psycho-analytic variety. Such an appeal can certainly not be explained in any conventional literary critical terms, yet it is there for readers of all ages, and in a form that might only have been possible because Carroll originally thought of the story in terms of a child audience.

The Wind in the Willows is another example perhaps of this particular genre: a story first told and later written for children that also has something enduring in it for the adult imagination too. Again, everyone knows the simple story; how can one explain the appeal? For Peter Green, in his biography *Kenneth Grahame,*** the story voices some of the author's own fear about a threatened social order, with the upper class

* Martin Gardner (ed.), *The Annotated Alice* (Penguin, 1965).

** Peter Green, *Kenneth Grahame, a Study of His Life, Work and Times* (Murray, 1959).

river dwellers, all straw hats and picnic hampers, under perpetual danger from h-dropping and insanitary vermin from the Wild Wood just outside. Others have seen the story differently, as a fantasy about the simple life, where humanised animals, without any of the sexual or economic problems of human existence, live in happiness and innocence: an Arcadia that has always played a part in human myth-making. In an essay later on in this book I shall discuss more ways in which one might see the character of Toad. Different interpretations need not necessarily be counter-exclusive, but rather an indication of the richness of the work and of an appeal, once again, that defies orthodox logic or literary criticism.

At this point it could be argued that whilst children's literature may have an attractive, overt fantasy component, this is something shared by all literature, although often in less obvious ways. *Oliver Twist,* for example, whilst about the Poor Law, villainy and London street life is also, at another level, in the long tradition of the ever-popular Cinderella situation, where the poorest become the richest via fairy godmother, forged will or whatever. Other popular, recurrent fantasies of this sort, such as the beauty who must appear as a beast, crop up in world mythology and popular fiction over and over again. To say, then, that children's literature may have a large share of this mythopoeic quality, is not to deny that many adult novels, from *Jane Eyre* to *Silas Marner* may equally take some of their roots from the same type of fantasy.

If one accepts this argument, it would also seem true that writers of fiction for adults today tend to be much less generous in this sort of area than before. Adults and children could read each other's books far more easily in the 19th century, with novels like *Little Lord Fauntleroy* and *Great Expectations* sharing the same audience and, to an extent, the same fantasy. Today, the adult novel seems largely in retreat from the big theme and the universal, moralistic background. Writers prefer to deal with small areas of experience, often using a very fine brush. For this reason, it seems to me that children's literature has to a certain extent taken over from that sort of writing children can easily respond to, but which adults may also need, where popular, personal mythologies are represented at an uncomplicated level.

Take the picaresque novel, for example, a form of writing that has almost disappeared from the books of the best adult fiction writers today. Basically, this is yet another myth of the hero, starting out from small beginnings and defeating dangers on his way to maturity, or whatever particular symbol for this he is to find by the end of the story. Obviously, this story pattern has enormous attractions for children, as they too have to make this particular journey, and may want to test themselves out – at least in imagination – against some of the obstacles they can expect to meet. But adults can also be interested in such fiction; many of us still day-dream – a story about a perilous mission and a personal testing-out may continue to have attractions, even though it may have less relevance to normal adult life, increasingly pre-occupied with those unheroic, domestic details shunned in all good adventure stories.

Today, adults can no longer find this sort of literature at all easily at a level that is also critically satisfying, although, on a lower plane, popular best-selling authors continue to provide just these adventures, plus the sexual wish-fulfilment common in the picaresque story, along with other types of action. Many older children like this sort of writing too, and, typically, authors like Ian Fleming and Alistair MacLean have large audiences in both camps. James Bond is probably far more familiar to children than any other character drawn from fiction for whatever age-group.

There are, of course, multitudes of books written for children in this genre, but without the insistent dwelling on violence and sex that now characterises the popular paperback adventure story for adults. Some of this writing is of a high calibre, and authors who write adventures for a child audience may also incorporate other aspects more difficult to find in writing for adults, but still with a certain fascination for all age groups. For example, there is the whole world of magical thinking, talking animals and supernatural powers, shared by all children at a certain stage of their development, and perhaps never quite outgrown in the rest of us — thus the indestructibility of mild forms of superstition, horoscopes, interest in the occult and other popular resistance to logical thought. With a writer like Tolkien or, later, Ursula le Guin, readers can temporarily shelve the scientific, ordered world-view they have learned to develop over the years. Instead, they can exercise that other part of their thinking — the pre-logical, semi-mystical fantasy world that still plays a part in our lives, both in sleep and in wakefulness, but which is more neglected now in adult writing. A 19th century reader could still turn to fairy tales without much sense of indignity. The church, the Bible, or the whole more credulous, pre-social science world of rumour, tall-story or popular fad could still feed the remaining 'magical' aspects of thought, yet to be rendered less respectable by the growth of education at all stages. Today, the adult reader may find something of this in the world of science-fiction; elsewhere he can turn to a growing number of magico-adventure books originally published for children but soon taken over by the adult market too, from *The Hobbit* to Richard Adams' fine novel of talking rabbits, *Watership Down*.

But this type of overt fantasy is only part of children's literature; what of other, ostensibly more realistic works? In fact, I would suggest all children's literature shares a fantasy unrealistic element, even when the subject is at pains to be about life as it really is. For example, writing for a young audience usually implies cutting down on complexity, so that the main action never becomes confused by a profusion of incidental detail. Once again, this is a process to some extent common to 'all branches of fiction; as Henry James, no stranger to profusion or incidental detail, once pointed out: "Life is all inclusion and confusion, art is all discrimination and selection". This is so particularly true of children's fiction, although books for older readers may often blur many of the distinctions I am making here, sometimes to the extent of making it really impossible to say whether one is talking about recognisably children's books or not. But on the whole, characterisation in children's books offers fewer problems to the reader, with people more clearly labelled and acting more predictably than in real life. Again, something has to *happen* in a children's book; action cannot be suspended indefinitely for too much discussion of different possibilities. By the end, a situation may be more or less resolved, to the extent that the main characters will have come to terms with the main action, not always by coming out victor, but at least by seeing the position more clearly. Minor characters may also fit into an ending that makes moral sense, with small successes for the deserving, perhaps, and set-backs for the over-reaching. We leave such books, then, with a feeling that by and large things have worked out for the best, even though this may have involved pain for some of the book's characters *en route*.

Could this, then, be the prevalent fantasy that runs through all writing for children: that ultimately experience is manageable and amounts to something; that there are no loose ends in life and that in it there are lessons for all of us, if only we care to look? Such a formula also applies to much popular adult fiction, but a good or great writer for adults always has it in his power to pull the rug from under his audience, to lead the reader up what turns out to be a false, romantic trail, then to be confronted with some of life's less comforting realities. Here, things may not add up in the end, injustices may be multiplied rather than set to rights, the narrative – like life itself – may not even make perfect sense as it progresses. There may always be a tension in any fiction between what the reader wants for the characters and what the writer determines. Where adults are concerned, the writer can sometimes impose his own tragic or nihilistic vision on his audience, who will accept it out of respect for the truth or power of the experience the writer is offering. With children, at least in the West, to a certain extent impose their own mental patterns on the writer. If he steps too far away from the ordered way in which his audience view the world, he may well leave his readers behind altogether, something no author can afford to do.

This is not to say that children's writing must be made up of safe, moralistic stories always leading to a happy ending. Rather, it is more a question of atmosphere. In a children's book, the audience soon comes to feel that there is a firm, but not necessarily heavy hand on the tiller, guiding the reader through complexities and setting sail towards a resolution that is broadly going to make moral sense. Thus when set-backs or even tragedies occur, there is still that feeling that in the long run things will more or less work out, at least for the main characters. Adults who dip into this literature, therefore, may occasionally find that this tidying up of essential ambiguities rather patronising. On the other hand, when it is well done it can have all the force of a moral vision: the world as it should be.

All literature can share this quality, but in children's literature, I would suggest that the dénouement and 'message' tend to be more overt and positive than one could say for most literature. A great deal of popular drama has this quality too, especially on television; a phenomenon discussed by J.R. Goodlad in *A Sociology of Popular Drama** which analyses the strongly moralistic 'sermonising' quality of much peak-hour TV drama in some detail. It would be inaccurate, though, to suggest that it is only because of this particular outlook that children's books are popular with children or have something to offer adults by way of a change. Children may need a secure atmosphere in their books to feel secure themselves; adults may occasionally welcome a more direct appeal to their sympathies. But all this is background before which the children's writer has to prove himself by producing a really good story that will engage readers in its own right. In this respect, children's literature has a number of advantages.

* J.R. Goodlad, *A Sociology of Popular Drama* (Heinemann, 1971).

The permitted cutting down of ambiguities, the emphasis on action rather than on introspection, all lend themselves to stories that on the whole move fast with characters who are easily identifiable and have clear roles to play.

There are, of course, many types of writing available for children today. In nearly all of them, one will find that the child is the main character, and adults have subsidiary roles, although only immature writing pretends that they need hardly exist at all. In this way, the child reader can identify with the main action, and books become ways in which he explores himself and the world around him: his feelings, dilemmas and some of the situations he may soon face, or is already facing. Very simple books will put these situations simply; the more complex will merge into the adult novel, thus giving rise to that controversy beloved of conferences on children's literature: what is a children's book? In fact, this question usually applies only to the very top end of children's writing. Most books for younger children seem to me to fall quite easily outside adult interests, just as cruder, popular writing for children, such as that offered by the late Enid Blyton, has little to offer older age groups.

For the adult, the more complex children's book that I have discussed here, may have several things to offer. He may learn something about children, either through remembering his own childhood again, or else by re-living some of the situations a child may have to face, whether in life or in some of the books written for him. But more importantly, he may also get something out of the books for himself; he too may identify with the main action, not just as the child he once was, but as someone who is also engaged in the continuing human situation any good novel depicts, for whatever age group. In this sense, I am not going to say anything about techniques for getting children interested in books, or how to fit the book to the individual child. This is always a chancy business: there are so many good reasons why a child should or should not be interested in reading, depending on personality, social background, reading ability, family support, special interests and so on. But if there were one piece of advice I had to give teachers or parents concerned with this problem, it would be to value children's literature for its own sake. This is not to say adult readers can expect to get interested in everything; over-simplified books for the very young can be charming but hardly rivetting reading, and bad or dull books for any age are simply bad, dull books. But some authors, as I have tried to show, have something to offer all ages, and qualities not always available in other genres of fiction. If an adult can respond to this for himself, how much greater the chance that the children near him may think there is something in it for them too.

In the following sections of this book, I have collected together and introduced articles of interest to readers who want to go further in this field, particularly in some of the controversies, many of them quite old now, that can still be heard whenever the topic is discussed. In Part One, on fairy stories, I have included some attacks as well as defences of this particular genre, that has lasted so long and shows no sign of losing any of its popularity today. In Part Two, we consider the appeal of popular literature, in this case comics, whilst also taking up points that have been made against their occasional excesses. Part Three deals with fear in children's books, a topic that always seems of interest, though some of the more alarmist predictions of what literature is capable of doing to children have always seemed to me highly exaggerated. The fourth part looks at some favourite books for children, by way of considering some of their appeal and implications – in one case, asking whether there may not now be a case for letting one popular classic quietly disappear from library shelves. In the last section, I have included two general pieces of writing on aspects of children's literature, one by a talented children's author. I also include a short bibliography, for those interested in the further study of children's literature, always remembering that the best introduction to this fascinating subject is still, and always has been, to read the books themselves.

PART ONE
Fairy Stories

INTRODUCTION

Children enjoy fairy stories; many adults, over long periods of time, have worried about this. No one really knows where the most famous stories come from, except for those very few universal favourites that can be traced to an individual writer, such as Hans Andersen's *The Ugly Duckling*. For the rest, however, their origin is a mystery, and a major source of controversy to 19th century folk-lorists. Were they originally dispersed from a common source in Indian culture by talkative merchants travelling from port to port? If not, how did so many different cultures come to share the same stories, however separated geographically? Or could it be that the stories dealt with physical phenomena common to all cultures, so that the bright-haired Cinderella becomes a myth about the dawn hidden by dark clouds in the night (the step-mother and ugly sisters) but rescued by the sun — and prince — in the morning? Later, when this theory too was discredited, psycho-analysts had an alternative variation: fairy tales reflected the common psychic battles of every child in a family. *Cinderella* is really about the jealousy a girl feels for her mother and sisters in the battle for her father's love.

There were still other arguments and approaches. The Grimm brothers researched into fairy tales in an effort to piece together a common Teutonic past that once united all the German-speaking races. When they first published their tales, it was as a scholarly piece of research, plus footnotes. Children seized on them, however, forcing reprint after reprint, as well as progressive modifications of the original stories in favour of a younger audience. But long before this, moralists had been worried about the possible effects of hearing such tales, which even if not in print, could still enter the nursery by story-telling, from the servants if not from the parents. Did such stories set a good moral example? Were they filling children's heads with ideas of magic, instead of introducing useful reality at an early age? Traces of this concern can still be found today; Maria Montessori discouraged her students from telling fairy stories to children under four, and contemporary Women's Liberation groups have found some fairy tales appallingly sexist. In Simone de Beauvoir's words, "Woman is the Sleeping Beauty, Cinderella, Snow White, she who receives, submits".*

All sorts of arguments will no doubt continue, but what perhaps should have been learned by now is that fairy tales are powerful stuff. Their appeal over the centuries, whatever it consists of — and there are numerous speculations — has been very strong. Those who tamper with them too overtly, and many have tried, generally end up looking silly. Those who try banning them altogether seldom have any greater success; it has been claimed that children are able to invent something like their own fairy stories, either in dreams or fantasy, whether they have ever heard such stories before or not.

Mrs Trimmer, quoted in the first extract, was an early objector to fairy stories. Her arguments may seem self-righteous, even ridiculous now, but it would be a mistake to over-patronise her. In contrast to many others at the time, she always took the whole idea of childhood seriously, and was also a tough campaigner for children's rights, founding her own school for the very young who would otherwise have had nothing except workshop or neglect. She was also an early protester against cruelty to animals, which again should not be mistaken for sentimentality. The abuses she wrote against make sickening reading now.

In 1802 she founded a magazine, *The Guardian of Education,* which, amongst other things, carried the first regular reviews of children's literature. The aim was "to contribute to the preservation of the young and innocent from the

* Simone de Beauvoir, *The Second Sex,* p.294 (Penguin, 1972).

32

dangers which threaten them in the form of infantine and juvenile literature". If any children's book had a strong moral, it might be favourably reviewed, but fun — as with so many moralists — was seen as more subversive, hence the condemnation of *John Gilpin*. Later, Mrs Trimmer became more dubious about fairy tales, even if there was nothing actually discreditable about the plot. On more rational grounds, was it really useful reading about anything other than the stern truth?

This may seem excessive concern now, but our own contemporary moralists are not always so very different, although they have learned to present their arguments rather more subtly. Mrs Trimmer obviously knew little child psychology; although it may have been a fair assumption at the time she was writing to imagine that a child might respond immediately to any bad message in whatever book. Even now, this is still an arguable point. Her warnings against the possible bad effects of reading *Robinson Crusoe* are not so different from our own worries over youthful audiences viewing violent films. And her criticism of the illustrations to a particular edition of *Bluebeard* do not seem unreasonable; adult sadism in books for the young is a quite legitimate cause for concern or dislike.

But if a few of the points Mrs Trimmer once made are still worth discussion, even in her own time she was already fighting a losing battle. Her own feelings of nostalgia for some of the old stories, briefly alluded to before she went on to condemn them, were also shared by many others but without her particular moral concern. Some of the greatest allies of fairy stories have always been those adults, like Dr Johnson, who remember reading them when young, and subsequently demand to know what possible harm they might have done — the same argument that can justify corporal punishment, boarding schools, bullying, or indeed almost anything that can happen to a child. Contemporary fiction, of course, cannot use such allies until its readers have themselves become parents, which may partially explain a backwards-looking tendency that has always run through discussion about children's literature.

The great illustrator, George Cruikshank, was another who worried over the bad effects of some fairy tales, and in his case I have included extracts from his own improved versions. These came about when Cruikshank was originally asked to illustrate Cinderella. On taking up the text, however, "I found *some* vulgarity, mixed up with so much that was useless and unfit for children, that I was obliged, (much against my wish) to rewrite the whole story". The result, added to Cruikshank's fervent belief in teetotalism, is somewhat startling. Cinderella is always something of a passive heroine; here, in dialogue with her fairy god-mother, she becomes positively embarrassing.

"Why Cindy, my darling, you have been crying?"

"Yes", she replied with a sweet smile, "I did shed a few tears when I saw my sisters going to the Royal Ball; and I thought that I should like, above all things, to go; but the thought of my poor father came to my mind, and I now feel that I should not like to go and enjoy myself and be merry, whilst my poor father is pining in prison".

Cruikshank's ending to this story should be a warning to any who try to rewrite traditional material too drastically, and the last moments of *Jack and the Beanstalk,* also included, offer another bizarre insight into the Victorian ideal of useful toil; how much more sensible, and economical, to make the Giant work rather than simply allow him to crash to death at the foot of the beanstalk. Cruikshank's illustration at this point shows the Giant looking very much like an outsize navvy, the implication perhaps that all working class drunkards should be firmly but kindly redirected, or should it be 're-cycled', in this way.

Cruikshank's eventual *Fairy Library,* comprising four re-written tales in all, invited ridicule even at the time, and this duly came from Dickens, at his most biting. I have included his essay 'Frauds on the Fairies' as a witty piece of invective that is still relevant today. There have always been attempted encroachments on children's literature, and in our own time dentists have objected to sweet-eating in books, feminists to sexism, socialists to middle-class backgrounds, and others to Billy Bunter (making fun of obesity) Biggles (racism) and Enid Blyton (almost everything from encouraging children to be impertinent to adults to inculcating social snobbishness at every possible level). Clearly it is absurd to lump all these criticisms together; each must be taken on its own merits. But I think that the example Dickens sets here, is still a useful one to remember against many of those who wish to interfere with the freedom of literature and the reader, without really having given the whole matter very much thought.

A more thoughtful critique of fairy tales is offered in the next extract by Dr Langfeldt. As he says, such stories have always shown the darker side of mankind, and only a fanatic would wish to preserve every resurrected folk-tale for children, even those the Grimm brothers themselves dropped as too horrifying. All collections of fairy tales represent someone's *selection* from the past, and the finished product is always far more literary in style than the original oral source could ever have been. It is a mistake to think that any popular folk-lorist, from the Grimm brothers to Joseph Jacobs and Andrew Lang, ever wrote down such stories exactly as they heard them. So the search for the 'pure' fairy story, uncensored and truly representative of an original, oral culture, is probably something of a myth, so far as published children's editions are concerned.

How far should our selectors and re-writers go? Dr Langfeldt sees the story of *Hansel and Gretel* as giving a young reader "a severe shock". But could this be one of the functions of fairy tales — to inform young people about the totality of human beings, the capacity for good and evil in all of us — reader or writer? In *A Bridge of Children's Books,** Jella Lepman describes setting up an exhibition of children's books in Germany just after the last war. "Once an old woman leading a child by the hand asked me, "Aren't there any books of fairy tales without *Hansel and Gretel?* . . . The child's

* Jella Lepman, *A Bridge of Children's Books,* p.56 (Brockhampton, 1969).

parents died in Auschwitz, in the gas chambers. . .Yes, in the witch's oven. The child was in the camp herself, and escaped only by a miracle."

Is the witch's oven prophetic, a warning to us, or an encouragement to imitation, along with some of the other casual cruelty in these fairy tales? Or could it be that fairy stories are a treasure trove; and that what readers do with the treasure may depend upon them as much as on what they find? But finally, on the very real riches that are in these stories, I have included an article by Catherine Storr.

MRS TRIMMER
from *The Guardian of Education*

The renowned History of a White Cat, and other interesting Stories. Newbery.

Those who indulge children with reading fairy tales, will approve of the History of the White Cat, which is taken from some French work. The story of Miss Johnson is an improving one; and the History of the Golden Head has a moral, which probably children will comprehend.

The History of Beasts and Birds, with a familiar Description of each, in Verse and Prose, by Tommy Trip; to which is prefixed the History of the Author, and his little Dog Jowler. Newbery.

This little volume answers to its title page; it is a pleasing epitome of natural history, with prints of a variety of birds and beasts.

The History of John Gilpin, a droll Story, and the Ballad of the Children of the Wood. Price 4d. Glasgow. Lumsden and Son.

We have here one of the productions of the *Toy-Book Manufactory in Scotland,* but which we cannot recommend to the children of *South Britain,* as we do not think the materials of which it is composed proper for Children's Books. The poem of *John Gilpin* places an honest, industrious trades-man, worthy to be held out as an example of prudence and economy to men of his rank, in a ridiculous situation, and provokes a laugh at the expence of conjugal affection. The *Droll Story* relates to the propagation of a lie, or rather the magnifying a simple report into a reiterated falsehood, the drift of which children could not understand. The story of the *Coach and Dung Cart* is equally unintelligible to them. That of the *Elephant and the Taylor* is to be met with in twenty other books; and the ballad of the *Children in the Wood* is absolutely unfit for the perusal of children: nor do we think they would comprehend the *Proverbs*.

(Volume I, May-December 1802.)

Mother Bunch's Fairy Tales. Price 6d. Newbery.

Partial, as we confess ourselves to be, to most of the books of the old school, we cannot approve of those which are only fit to fill the heads of children with confused notions of wonderful and supernatural events, brought about by the agency of imaginary beings. *Mother Bunch's Tales* are of this description.

Histories and Tales of Past Times, told by Mother Goose. Price 6d.

Though we well remember the interest with which, in our childish days, when books of amusement for children were scarce, we read, or listened to the history of *Little Red Riding Hood*, and *Blue Beard*, &c. we do not wish to have such sensations awakened in the hearts of our grandchildren, by the same means; for the terrific images, which tales of this nature present to the imagination, usually make deep impressions, and injure the tender minds of children, by exciting unreasonable and groundless fears. Neither do the generality of tales of this kind supply any moral instruction level to the infantine capacity.

(Volume II, January-August 1803.)

The Life and strange surprising Adventures of Robinson Crusoe, of York, Mariner, who lived eight and twenty years alone in an uninhabited Island. Written by himself. In two volumes.

This work has gone through a surprising number of large editions, and in respect to its general merits we believe it to be the universal opinion, that it is one of the most interesting and entertaining books that was ever written: nor is it destitute of important instruction; for it exhibits in a most striking light the power with which the human mind is endued, to relieve the wants of the body; and to sustain the evils of life with fortitude and resignation under the most distressing circumstances. On these accounts the life of Robinson Crusoe, has been employed in the education of boys, for the purpose of shewing what ingenuity and industry can effect, under the divine blessing. But a question has arisen whether this book should be put into the hands of *all boys* without discrimination. Our opinion is, that it ought not, for children of very lively imaginations, and accustomed to indulge their fancy without control in their infantine amusements, may undoubtedly, be led by it, into an early taste for a rambling life, and a desire of adventures: an instance of this was related to us as a fact. Two little boys in consequence of reading the History of Robinson Crusoe, set off together from their parents' houses, in order to embark in some ship, with the hope of being cast on an uninhabited island; and though they certainly did not succeed in their project, it was productive of fatal effects, for the mother of one of them during the time they were missing, was, in consequence of anxiety of mind, seized with an illness which shortly put a period to her days. Caution, therefore, in respect to the temper and disposition of a child ought to be used, before a work of so fascinating a nature is put into his hands; but where the mind and temper have been properly regulated, it may be safely used as a stimulus to mental and bodily exertion, and patient perseverance.

(Volume III, July 1804.)

Nursery Tales. Cinderella, Blue Beard, and Little Red Riding Hood; with coloured plates. Price 6d. each. Tabart. 1804.

These Tales are announced to the public as *new translations,* but in what respect this term applies we are at a loss to say, for, on the perusal of them we recognized the identical *Mother Goose's Tales,* with all their *vulgarities of expression,* which were in circulation when those who are now grandmothers, were themselves children, and we doubt not but that many besides ourselves can recollect, their horrors of imagination on reading that of *Blue Beard,* and the terrific impressions it left upon their minds. This is certainly a very improper tale for children. *Cinderella* and *Little Red Riding Hood* are perhaps merely absurd. But it is not on account of their subjects and language only that these Tales, (*Blue Beard* at least) are exceptionable, another objection to them arises from the nature of their embellishments, consisting of coloured prints, in which the most striking incidents in the stories are placed before the eyes of the little readers in glaring colours, representations we believe of play-house scenes, (for the figures are in theatrical dresses). In *Blue Beard* for instance, the second plate represents the opening of the *forbidden closet,* in which appears, not what the story describes, (which surely is *terrific enough!) "a floor clotted with blood, in which the bodies of several women were lying (the wives whom Blue Beard had married and murdered,")* but, *the flames of Hell* with *Devils* in frightful shapes, threatening the unhappy lady who had given way to her curiosity! The concluding print is, *Blue Beard* holding his terrified wife by the hair, and lifting up his sabre to cut off her head. We expected in *Little Red Riding Hood,* to have found a picture of the wolf tearing the poor innocent dutiful child to pieces, but happily the number of prints was complete without it. A moment's consideration will surely be sufficient to convince people of the least reflection, of the danger, as well as the impropriety, of putting such books as these into the hands of little children, whose minds are susceptible of every impression; and who from the liveliness of their imaginations are apt to convert into realities whatever forcibly strikes their fancy.

(Volume IV, January 1805.)

GEORGE CRUIKSHANK
from *Cinderella*

. . . the father mounted the horse upon which he had returned home; and, with the herald, trumpeters, and chamberlain in front, and the father, followed by the guards in the rear, they proceeded towards the royal palace, accompanied by a large concourse of people, who were in a state of great excitement, and kept on shouting until the cavalcade reached the palace, at the gates of which the Prince was waiting to receive Cinderella, which he did with great delight. He was somewhat surprised at the appearance of the dwarf; but when Cinderella informed him that she was her godmother and her best friend, he saluted the little lady with great respect, and conducted them both to the Queen his mother. Cinderella had also presented her father to the Prince, whom he welcomed most cordially, desiring his page in waiting to conduct him to his own apartments, where he soon joined him to say that the King, his father, wished to have an interview. They accordingly repaired to the royal library, where they found his Majesty, attended by his chancellor and other law-officers. The King was delighted to find an old friend in the person of Cinderella's father, who, as may be supposed, readily gave his consent to the marriage of his daughter to the Prince; and the lawyers having drawn up the marriage-contract, they all repaired to the Queen's apartments, to have it signed by Cinderella, the Royal Prince, and the other parties.

The Queen had been in conversation with the dwarf, and was so much pleased with her wit and good sense, that she introduced her to the King's especial notice, who received Cinderella's godmother with great condescension and affability. It was determined that the marriage should take place as soon as the necessary preparations could be made; "That is," his Majesty jocosely said, "if it met with the approbation of the young people." The Prince smilingly replied, that they would be guided by his Majesty's pleasure.

The King, who was in the highest flow of spirits, declared that there should be extraordinary grand doings to celebrate this wedding; and, amongst other things, ordered that there should be running "fountains of wine" in the court-yards of the palace, and also in the streets. Upon which Cinderella's godmother, who had been conversing with the King, begged that his Majesty would not carry out that part of the arrangements.

"Why not?" said the King; "it is the custom upon all great festive occasions, and the people would be disappointed were it omitted at a royal wedding."

"It is true," replied the dwarf, "that the people look for such things, but although there is much boisterous mirth created by the drink around these wine fountains, yet your Majesty is aware that this same drink leads also to quarrels, brutal fights, and violent deaths."

"Well! I fear it is so," the King replied; "but this misconduct and violence is only committed by those who take *too much,* and not by those who take it in moderation."

"The history of the use of strong drinks," the dwarf said, "is marked on every page by *excess, which follows, as a matter of course, from the very nature of their composition,* and are always accompanied by ill-health, misery, and crime."

"Well, but," said the King, "what is to be done? are not these things intended by Providence for our use?"

"With all deference to your Majesty," said the dwarf in reply, "most assuredly not; for such is the POWER of the CREATOR, that if it had been necessary for man to take stimulating drinks, the ALMIGHTY could have given them to him *free from all intoxicating qualities,* as he has done with all solids and liquids necessary and fit for the support of man's life; and as he never intended that any man should be intoxicated, and as he knows that all men cannot take these drinks alike, *such is his goodness and mercy,* THAT HE WOULD HAVE SENT THEM TO US WITHOUT THE INTOXICATING PRINCIPLE; and when people talk of these intoxicating drinks, that do so much deadly mischief, being *sent* to us by the ALMIGHTY, we might as well say that he sends us gunpowder, because man converts certain materials into such a deadly composition. And as *to moderation,* pardon me, your Majesty, but so long as your Majesty continues to take even half a glass of wine a-day, so long will the drinking customs of society be considered respectable and kept up; and it thus follows, as a necessary consequence, that thousands of your Majesty's subjects will be constantly falling by *excess* into *vice, wretchedness, and crime;* and as to people not being able to do without stimulating drinks, I beg your Majesty to look at Cinderella, who never has taken any in all her life, and who never will."

"My dear little lady," exclaimed the King, good-humouredly, "your arguments have convinced me: there shall be no more fountains of wine in my dominions." And he immediately gave orders that all the wine, beer, and spirits, in the place, should be collected together and piled upon the top of a rocky mound in the vicinity of the palace, and made a great bonfire of on the night of the wedding; —which was accordingly done, and a splendid blaze it made!

An early day was then fixed for the wedding, which was solemnised in the cathedral with great pomp and splendour, all the great people in the country being present, including, of course, Cinderella's father and her mother-in-law. The King and Queen were seated upon a throne near the altar. Many beautiful young ladies attended Cinderella as bridemaids, amongst whom were her two sisters-in-law. The bride's dress was of the richest white satin, ornamented with bouquets of orange-blossoms; a large white lace veil covered her head; her brow was encircled with a wreath of orange-blossoms, mixed with diamonds, whose sparkles seemed dimmed by the brightness of her beautiful blue eyes; and her long, waving, and clustering ringlets shadowed the rosy blush of her lovely face. A number of beautiful little girls, dressed in white, carrying baskets containing flowers, preceded Cinderella and the Royal Prince, her handsome bridegroom, and who strewed their path with flowers as they approached the altar.

After the marriage there was a magnificent banquet, and festivities upon the grandest scale were kept up for several days. And they all lived to a great age in happiness and comfort.

(From *The Fairy Library,* 1853.)

from *Jack and the Beanstalk*

. . . The King was much pleased with Jack, and surprised that such a little fellow should have achieved so much and so well, and giving him a handsome jewel as a mark of his regard, desired that when he was a little older, he would come to the Court and be one of his pages. A Council was then held as to what was to be done with the Giant—whether he was to be killed or kept prisoner. Jack's mother, out of gratitude to the Giantess for having saved her life and the lives of her children, and indeed, as it appeared, her husband's life also, prayed the King to spare the Giant's life.

King Alfred granted her petition, and being a wise king, he determined to turn such great strength to some useful purpose, and therefore placed him under guard in the royal quarries, to hew out great stones for building royal and public places. The Giant's wife was allowed to live with him, and as he never had any intoxicating liquor to get tipsy with, he never beat or ill-used her any more, and they lived happily for many years.

After Jack's father and mother got settled, and the castle put in order, the Flower Fairy, the Hen, and the Harp, lent their aid to make it one of the happiest of homes—a happiness more felt in contrast to the adversity they had suffered.

On the evening of the day before Jack's father, mother, sister, and himself, left the valley with the Giant, his father gave a great feast to all the inhabitants of the place, to pay for which the Golden Hen was so good as to lay, on that morning, an extraordinary number of golden eggs, which found a ready market.

(From *The Fairy Library,* 1853.)

46

CHARLES DICKENS
Frauds on the Fairies

We may assume that we are not singular in entertaining a
very great tenderness for the fairy literature of our childhood.
What enchanted us then, and is captivating a million of young
fancies now, has, at the same blessed time of life, enchanted
vast hosts of men and women who have done their long day's
work, and laid their grey heads down to rest. It would be hard
to estimate the amount of gentleness and mercy that has
made its way among us through these slight channels. For-
bearance, courtesy, consideration for the poor and aged, kind
treatment of animals, the love of nature, abhorrence of
tyranny and brute force—many such good things have been
first nourished in the child's heart by this powerful aid. It
has greatly helped to keep us, in some sense, ever young, by
preserving through our wordly ways one slender track not
overgrown with weeds, where we may walk with children,
sharing their delights.

In an utilitarian age, of all other times, it is a matter of
grave importance that Fairy tales should be respected. Our
English red tape is too magnificently red ever to be employed in the tying up of such trifles, but every one who has
considered the subject knows full well that a nation without
fancy, without some romance, never did, never can, never
will, hold a great place under the sun. The theatre, having
done its worst to destroy these admirable fictions—and having
in a most exemplary manner destroyed itself, its artists, and
its audiences, in that perversion of its duty—it becomes doubly
important that the little books themselves, nurseries of fancy
as they are, should be preserved. To preserve them in their
usefulness, they must be as much preserved in their

simplicity, and purity, and innocent extravagance, as if they were actual fact. Whosoever alters them to suit his own opinions, whatever they are, is guilty, to our thinking, of an act of presumption, and appropriates to himself what does not belong to him.

We have lately observed, with pain, the intrusion of a Whole Hog of unwieldy dimensions into the fairy flower garden. The rooting of the animal among the roses would in itself have awakened in us nothing but indignation; our pain arises from his being violently driven in by a man of genius, our own beloved friend, MR. GEORGE CRUIK-SHANK. That incomparable artist is, of all men, the last who should lay his exquisite hand on fairy text. In his own art he understands it so perfectly, and illustrates it so beautifully, so humorously, so wisely, that he should never lay down his etching needle to "edit" the Ogre, to whom with that little instrument he can render such extraordinary justice. But, to "editing" Ogres, and Hop-o'-my-thumbs, and their families, our dear moralist has in a rash moment taken, as a means of propagating the doctrines of Total Abstinence, Prohibition of the sale of spirituous liquors, Free Trade, and Popular Education. For the introduction of these topics, he has altered the text of a fairy story; and against his right to do any such thing we protest with all our might and main. Of his likewise altering it to advertise that excellent series of plates, "The Bottle," we say nothing more than that we foresee a new and improved edition of *Goody Two Shoes,* edited by E. Moses and Son; of the *Dervish* with the box of ointment, edited by Professor Holloway; and of *Jack and the Beanstalk,* edited by Mary Wedlake, the popular authoress of *Do you bruise your oats yet.*

Now, it makes not the least difference to our objection whether we agree or disagree with our worthy friend, Mr. Cruikshank, in the opinions he interpolates upon an old fairy story. Whether good or bad in themselves, they are, in that relation, like the famous definition of a weed; a thing growing up in a wrong place. He has no greater moral justification in altering the harmless little books than we should have in altering his best etchings. If such a precedent were followed we must soon become disgusted with the old stories into which modern personages so obtruded themselves, and the stories themselves must soon be lost. With seven Blue Beards in the field, each coming at a gallop from his own platform mounted on a foaming hobby, a generation or two hence would not know which was which, and the great original Blue Beard would be confounded with the counterfeits. Imagine a Total abstinence edition of *Robinson Crusoe,* with the rum left out. Imagine a Peace edition, with the gunpowder left out, and the rum left in. Imagine a Vegetarian edition, with the goat's flesh left out. Imagine a Kentucky edition, to introduce a flogging of that 'tarnal old nigger Friday, twice a week. Imagine an Aborigines Protection Society edition, to deny the cannibalism and make Robinson embrace the amiable savages whenever they landed. *Robinson Crusoe* would be "edited" out of his island in a hundred years, and the island would be swallowed up in the editorial ocean.

Among the other learned professions we have now the Platform profession, chiefly exercised by a new and meritorious class of commercial travellers who go about to take the sense of meetings on various articles: some, of a very superior description: some, not quite so good. Let us write the story of *Cinderella,* "edited" by one of these gentlemen, doing a good stroke of business, and having a rather extensive mission.

Once upon a time, a rich man and his wife were the parents of a lovely daughter. She was a beautiful child, and became, at her own desire, a member of the Juvenile Bands of Hope when she was only four years of age. When this child was only nine years of age her mother died, and all the Juvenile Bands of Hope in her district—the Central district, number five hundred and twenty-seven—formed in a procession of two and two, amounting to fifteen hundred, and followed her to the grave, singing chorus Number forty-two, "O come,"

&c. This grave was outside the town, and under the direction of the Local Board of Health, which reported at certain stated intervals to the General Board of Health, Whitehall.

The motherless little girl was very sorrowful for the loss of her mother, and so was her father too, at first; but, after a year was over, he married again—a very cross widow lady, with two proud tyrannical daughters as cross as herself. He was aware that he could have made his marriage with this lady a civil process by simply making a declaration before a Registrar; but he was averse to this course on religious grounds, and, being a member of the Montgolfian persuasion, was married according to the ceremonies of that respectable church by the Reverend Jared Jocks, who improved the occasion.

He did not live long with his disagreeable wife. Having been shamefully accustomed to shave with warm water instead of cold, which he ought to have used (see Medical Appendix B. and C.), his undermined constitution could not bear up against her temper, and he soon died. Then, this orphan was cruelly treated by her stepmother and the two daughters, and was forced to do the dirtiest of the kitchen work; to scour the saucepans, wash the dishes, and light the fires—which did not consume their own smoke, but emitted a dark vapour prejudicial to the bronchial tubes. The only warm place in the house where she was free from ill-treatment was the kitchen chimney-corner; and as she used to sit down there, among the cinders, when her work was done, the proud fine sisters gave her the name of Cinderella.

About this time, the King of the land, who never made war against anybody, and allowed everybody to make war against him—which was the reason why his subjects were the greatest manufacturers on earth, and always lived in security and peace—gave a great feast, which was to last two days. This splendid banquet was to consist entirely of artichokes and gruel; and from among those who were invited to it, and to hear the delightful speeches after dinner, the King's son was to choose a bride for himself. The proud fine sisters were invited, but nobody knew anything about poor Cinderella, and she was to stay at home.

She was so sweet-tempered, however, that she assisted the haughty creatures to dress, and bestowed her admirable taste upon them as freely as if they had been kind to her. Neither did she laugh when they broke seventeen stay-laces in dressing; for, although she wore no stays herself, being sufficiently acquainted with the anatomy of the human figure to be aware of the destructive effects of tight-lacing, she always reserved her opinions on that subject for the Regenerative Record (price three halfpence in a neat wrapper), which all good people take in, and to which she was a Contributor.

At length the wished for moment arrived, and the proud fine sisters swept away to the feast and speeches, leaving Cinderella in the chimney-corner. But, she could always occupy her mind with the general question of the Ocean Penny Postage, and she had in her pocket an unread Oration on that subject, made by the well known Orator, Nehemiah Nicks. She was lost in the fervid eloquence of that talented Apostle when she became aware of the presence of one of those female relatives which (it may not be generally known) it is not lawful for a man to marry. I allude to her grandmother.

"Why so solitary, my child?" said the old lady to Cinderella.

"Alas, grandmother," returned the poor girl, "my sisters have gone to the feast and speeches, and here sit I in the ashes, Cinderella!"

"Never," cried the old lady with animation, "shall one of the Band of Hope despair! Run into the garden, my dear, and fetch me an American Pumpkin! American, because in some parts of that independent country, there are prohibitory laws against the sale of alcoholic drinks in any form. Also; because America produced (among many great pumpkins) the glory of her sex, Mrs. Colonel Bloomer. None but an American Pumpkin will do, my child."

Cinderella ran into the garden, and brought the largest American Pumpkin she could find. This virtuously democratic vegetable her grandmother immediately changed into a

51

splendid coach. Then, she sent her for six mice from the mouse-trap, which she changed into prancing horses, free from the obnoxious and oppressive post-horse duty. Then, to the rat-trap in the stable for a rat, which she changed to a state-coachman, not amenable to the iniquitous assessed taxes. Then, to look behind a watering-pot for six lizards, which she changed into six footmen, each with a petition in his hand ready to present to the Prince, signed by fifty thousand persons, in favour of the early closing movement.

"But grandmother," said Cinderella, stopping in the midst of her delight, and looking at her clothes, "how can I go to the palace in these miserable rags?"

"Be not uneasy about that, my dear," returned her grandmother.

Upon which the old lady touched her with her wand, her rags disappeared, and she was beautifully dressed. Not in the present costume of the female sex, which has been proved to be at once grossly immodest and absurdly inconvenient, but in rich sky-blue satin pantaloons gathered at the ankle, a puce-colored satin pelisse sprinkled with silver flowers, and a very broad Leghorn hat. The hat was chastely ornamented with a rainbow-coloured ribbon hanging in two bell-pulls down the back; the pantaloons were ornamented with a golden stripe; and the effect of the whole was unspeakably sensible, feminine, and retiring. Lastly, the old lady put on Cinderella's feet a pair of shoes made of glass; observing that but for the abolition of the duty on that article, it never could have been devoted to such a purpose; the effect of all such taxes being to cramp invention, and embarrass the producer, to the manifest injury of the consumer. When the old lady had made these wise remarks, she dismissed Cinderella to the feast and speeches, charging her by no means to remain after twelve o'clock at night.

The arrival of Cinderella at the Monster Gathering produced a great excitement. As a delegate from the United States had just moved that the King do take the chair, and as the motion had been seconded and carried unanimously, the King himself could not go forth to receive her. But His Royal Highness the Prince (who was to move the second resolution), went to the door to hand her from her carriage. This virtuous Prince, being completely covered from head to foot with Total Abstinence Medals, shone as if he were attired in complete armour; while the inspiring strains of the Peace Brass Band in the gallery (composed of the Lambkin Family, eighteen in number, who cannot be too much encouraged) awakened additional enthusiasm.

The King's son handed Cinderella to one of the reserved seats for pink tickets on the platform, and fell in love with her immediately. His appetite deserted him; he scarcely tasted his artichokes, and merely trifled with his gruel. When the speeches began, and Cinderella, wrapped in the eloquence of the two inspired delegates who occupied the entire evening in speaking to the first Resolution, occasionally cried, "Hear, hear!" the sweetness of her voice completed her conquest of the Prince's heart. But, indeed the whole male portion of the assembly loved her—and doubtless would have done so, even if she had been less beautiful, in consequence of the contrast which her dress presented to the bold and ridiculous garments of the other ladies.

At a quarter before twelve the second inspired delegate having drunk all the water in the decanter, and fainted away, the King put the question, "That this Meeting do now adjourn until to-morrow." Those who were of that opinion holding up their hands, and then those who were of the contrary, theirs, there appeared an immense majority in favour of the resolution, which was consequently carried. Cinderella got home in safety, and heard nothing all that night or all next day, but the praises of the unknown lady with the sky-blue satin pantaloons.

When the time for the feast and speeches came round again, the cross stepmother and the proud fine daughters went out in good time to secure their places. As soon as they were gone, Cinderella's grandmother returned and changed her as before. Amid a blast of welcome from the Lambkin family, she was again handed to the pink seat on the platform by His Royal Highness.

This gifted Prince was a powerful speaker, and had the evening before him. He rose at precisely ten minutes before eight, and was greeted with tumultuous cheers and waving of handkerchiefs. When the excitement had in some degree subsided, he proceeded to address the meeting; who were never tired of listening to speeches, as no good people ever are. He held them enthralled for four hours and a quarter. Cinderella forgot the time, and hurried away so when she heard the first stroke of twelve, that her beautiful dress changed back to her old rags at the door, and she left one of her glass shoes behind. The Prince took it up, and vowed—that is, made a declaration before a magistrate; for he objected on principle to the multiplying of oaths—that he would only marry the charming creature to whom that shoe belonged.

He accordingly caused an advertisement to that effect to be inserted in all the newspapers; for, the advertisement duty, an impost most unjust in principle and most unfair in operation, did not exist in that country; neither was the stamp on newspapers known in that land—which had as many newspapers as the United States, and got as much good out of them. Innumerable ladies answered this advertisement and pretended that the shoe was theirs; but, every one of them was unable to get her foot into it. The proud fine sisters answered it, and tried their feet with no greater success. Then, Cinderella, who had answered it too, came forward amidst their scornful jeers, and the shoe slipped on in a moment. It is a remarkable tribute to the improved and sensible fashion of the dress her grandmother had given her, that if she had not worn it the Prince would probably never have seen her feet.

The marriage was solemnized with great rejoicing. When the honeymoon was over, the King retired from public life, and was succeeded by the Prince. Cinderella, being now a queen, applied herself to the government of the country on enlightened, liberal, and free principles. All the people who ate anything she did not eat, or who drank anything she did not drink, were imprisoned for life. All the newspaper offices from which any doctrine proceeded that was not her doctrine, were burnt down. All the public speakers proved to demonstration that if there were any individual on the face of the earth who differed from them in anything, that individual was a designing ruffian and an abandoned monster. She also threw open the right of voting, and of being elected to public offices, and of making the laws, to the whole of her sex; who thus came to be always gloriously occupied with public life and whom nobody dared to love. And they all lived happily ever afterwards.

Frauds on the Fairies once permitted, we see little reason why they may not come to this, and great reason why they may. The Vicar of Wakefield was wisest when he was tired of being always wise. The world is too much with us, early and late. Leave this precious old escape from it, alone.

(From *Household Words,* Number 184, October 1853.)

DR J. LANGFELDT
The Educational and Moral Values of Folk and Fairy Tales

After the war, when the Allies prepared for a re-education of the German people, one of their criticisms was that the German child, through excessive use of the German fables, especially of Grimms' folktales, had been brought up to take pleasure in representations of cruelty and also eventually educated in inhuman behaviour. It was said, for instance, that, especially in Grimms' Tales there were many stories in which horrifying traits were shown in human beings, making them truly bad examples for the young. Also that in many folktales encounters with monsters and horror-provoking figures made the child quite insensitive to coarse impressions. Criticisms were made of points which again and again during the two previous centuries had engaged and passionately excited German educationalists. One needs only to follow the discussion on fairy tales throughout the whole of the 19th century to come repeatedly upon the same or similar objections to the folk and fairy tales.

We know that the folk tale is centuries old, not only in Germany, but in all countries of the world. In early times these tales excited little critical notice, since they were not fixed in print, but only passed from mouth to mouth as "Old Wives' Tales," as they used to be called, especially during the 18th century. That fact made it not worthwhile to pay much attention to them, nor to their suitability for children's literature. The monster in the folktale was seen only as the nurse's exaggeration with which the children had to be frightened so that they would not run into the wood nor commit any other kind of error. Education by intimidation was at that time regarded as a perfectly justifiable means of ensuring correct behaviour among children. In consequence the "Mother Goose" tales, which Perrault published, were not examined so much for their horror, though in part the stories are far more frightening than the later Grimm stories. Think, for instance, of little Tom Thumb, who through exchange of headgear induces the seven-league-booted cannibal to kill his own children. These fairy tales made far less impression on adult consciousness than did the *Arabian Nights* which were translated shortly after and spread like wildfire throughout Europe, evoking a new style of fairy tale, which immediately appealed to adults. In Germany, the fairy tales told by Wieland, a friend of Goethe's and later a tutor to the Weimar princes, can be compared with them.

The 18th century, however, is the great century for education. One may think of the great influence of Locke's *Treatise on Education* on Rousseau, of Rousseau himself and of Pestalozzi. It is no wonder then that the great spirits of the century turned their attention to questioning the effect of the old wives' tales on the children. Among the outstanding intellects of the time in Germany was Herder who occupied himself for a long time with this question, and who instigated the publication of a collection of fairy tales – Palmblätter – by A.J. Liebeskind, tutor to his own children. In Herder's preface he says, "The soul of a child is sacred, and whatever is brought before it must have at least the merit of purity." Later, in his *Adrastea*, he expressed himself in still greater detail on his attitude towards the folk tales. "Have you read the "Mother Goose" stories?" everyone asks. "It would have been better, it seems to me, to have called them the "Father Gander Tales" for a Mother Goose would certainly have told something more suitable for her chicks . . . . What do children want with horrifying apparitions of bloodthirsty villains, wolves, ogres and such-like? The bestialities seem to be used solely to show up the timidity of the gosling so that it will cry, "The Wolf is Coming"; a mistaken aim for a fairy tale. Moreover, there is nothing more tasteless and more cruel than to spoil the imagination of a child through alarming and fraudulent figures. Whoever doubts the integrity of the child's soul should watch children when one tells them fairy tales. "No, that is not so," they say, "you told it me differently before." "I don't like that story; tell me another." I ask you, shall we offer innocent listeners figures of caricature, ugly spectres, which are valueless in themselves and have no connection with reality? Even the belief in an evil genius which travels with us as if to spoil our best intentions — even this belief seems hurtful to man's noble nature. The little Daemunculi in our own and other hearts ought never, even in fairy tales, to be the joint ruler of the universe or of our lives." Goethe was of a similar opinion, for he has never spoken much about Grimms' Tales though he has enlarged in detail over the Folk Song Collection of Arnim and Brentano. Brentano also was by no means enamoured of the first edition of Grimm, but disapproved of it, comparing it to a child's dirty dress. We know his interpretation of fairy tales exactly from his detailed treatment of Italian and Rhineland stories. Moreover, Arnim, in a lengthy correspondence with Wilhelm Grimm, again and again stressed that the fairy tales should be edited; and all his life W. Grimm polished and elaborated them. In the meantime, however, the spiritual and intellectual atmosphere had altered a great deal. Though Herder was the real originator of the German interest in the national folklore, at the same time his enthusiasm for everything popular and his spiritual and educational principles waged perpetual war in his mind, and the older he grew, the stronger became the pedagogue in him, since he was also responsible for the public education of Weimar.

With Arnim and Brentano, however, Romanticism triumphed and educational purposes were secondary to the enthusiasm for the national and popular. And so the criticism of Grimms' Tales was not characterised so much by educational scruples as by a determination to glorify people and fatherland. Critics were not shocked so much by the horrors of individual stories, but rather found them unsuitable to extol the national characteristics and folklore. The folk songs which they had published themselves were recast or manipulated to that end, if they did not correspond with their imaginative ideal. They had expected something similar from the folk tales and were now disappointed by the fidelity of the renderings. Jacob Grimm would not adapt himself to their criticism, but Wilhelm more and more tried to meet their demands.

It is therefore not surprising that in his later edition, we find not so much the pedagogue as the fine minded artist. No doubt he had omitted some of the stories which were really too frightful, e.g. "How children played at slaughtering," "The Okerlo," "The Castle of Murder." Again the mother in *Snow White* and in *Hansel and Gretel* became a stepmother. That Wilhelm Grimm did not concern himself so much with an educational approach can be particularly clearly seen in the ending of Cinderella. While we read in the first edition that after the discovery of the real bride, "the stepmother and the two proud sisters paled and became alarmed," we find in the later edition that both stepsisters were condemned to the dreadful punishment of having their eyes picked out by *doves,* whilst no mention is made of punishment of the stepmother. Here it is quite clear that aesthetic considerations directed Wilhelm Grimm's pen. The end must be fashioned – it must not be so colourless – everything must be quite clearly demonstrated.

It is a well known factor in the history of culture that the noble ideas of the great spirits gain ground only gradually. Therefore it is not surprising that the whole 19th century in the educational field was far from being ruled entirely by the ideas of the age of reason. And so in the next decade there was further public criticism of the educational deficiencies of Grimm's Tales. Above all there were complaints about the figure of the guilty stepmother. People thought this presentation of the stepmother in the folk tale an injustice to the many good stepmothers who, in fact, existed. But elsewhere, too, critical voices were raised amongst the educationists against the tales, through only slowly did their ideas have any effect.

At first with the movement towards æsthetic education, which coincided with the new romanticism of the 90's it was agreed that everything rooted in national folklore and character should be held to be more or less sacrosanct. So perhaps it was a good thing, when with the occupation of Germany, this question came once again to the fore. But the attitude taken up today is a little different from the way we understood it from Herder. We do not repudiate the monsters of the original edition so much *as such*. Giants and dwarfs, witches and trolls and dragons are met with everywhere in folk tales. That such monsters should be overcome in hard battles, that their heads should be struck off, all this corresponds absolutely with the child's feeling of justice. How easily it can be made harmless by suitable presentation is shown most convincingly in a little sketch by the Flemish writer Coolen, in which he relates how he tells folk tales to children. When a head is to be chopped off he accompanies such a statement with some such words as, "Smack, there he lay" and then the matter seems quite right to the children. They never realise what chopping a head off really means. As an example Coolen quotes *The Tinderbox* from Andersen, where the soldier strikes off the head of the witch, for whom he has fetched the tinderbox out of the hollow tree. Here are certainly no unheard-of horrors which could do harm to the listening children.

When we speak today of the questionable aspect of fairy tales, we think rather of other scenes. One of the weightiest objections can be raised against *Hansel and Gretel*. That parents, even when one is a stepmother, could decide to let their children starve in the woods, because there is no more food in the house, that seems from the psychological standpoint a completely impossible theme. Here harm can certainly be done to the child's mind; here a child can suffer a severe shock. The belief in their mothers, their parents, as the most certain support of their young lives, becomes suddenly uncertain and doubtful. Something similar results from the ending of Cinderella already quoted. That both sisters should be punished so severely, when their crimes are not really very great, whilst the evil stepmother is not punished at all – that must affect the child's feeling for justice very deeply, even though it lives in a moral world, with apparently firm standards.

Another example is *The Dog and the Sparrow.* The careless running down of the dog is an evil deed, but the vengeance taken by its friend, the sparrow, is so dreadful that one is not only reminded of the Old Testament "an eye for an eye, a tooth for a tooth" but in the end has to turn away in disgust from such vindictiveness. These are just a few examples of the objections that could be raised today against the thoughtless, universal dissemination of folk tales – objections which apply not only to the German folk tales.

But there is yet another side to this question which should be considered. In the excellent Belgian periodical, *Littérature de Jeunesse* was published a few years ago an article by the Belgian Profesor Dr. E. de Greff in which he says that there is another noteworthy aspect of the question of the rousing of fear through the folk tales. He points out that one of the most important points in education is the development of courage in the child. Just as the child must find courage to take its first steps away from its mother, so also it must learn to deal with other things which might cause it anxiety or fear. He then defends the folk tales with all their terrors. As an example he takes *Tom Thumb,* in Perrault's version. It is, one might say, a prototype of human development; that the child must break away from its parents in order to prove himself in the world with all its perils. Now it is well known that Perrault's version of *Tom Thumb* is particularly full of horrors. Tom Thumb, with his brothers, only escapes being devoured by the ogre because he exchanges headgear with the latter's daughters, and in consequence the ogre slays and devours his own children. I am not quite certain whether rather too much of youthful courage is not demanded here! It might be better, perhaps, instead of *Tom Thumb,* to consider Andersen's

Thumbling, who was also driven out into the world and there proved himself. But De Greff's general view and interpretation of the folk tales is correct. The tale is a journey, an adventure, in which a young person must take care of himself, in which he must be brave, in order to reach his goal. This approach gives a positive appraisal of the child's courage.

And here I should like to enlarge on Professor de Greff's theory. The child's bravery arises first from its consciousness of its security with its parents. This feeling, then, must not, as in *Hansel and Gretel,* be destroyed. On the other hand, however, a child's courage is based on its belief in the validity of moral law, in morality and in the power of love, as it has experienced it through its mother and its elders. And therefore in the fairy tales justice must be done; a punishment such as that of the sisters in Cinderella is inhuman; a revenge such as the sparrow takes is truly dreadful. Such experiences will not develop courage in the child. Therefore, we should not include tales of this kind in the collections for children.

But even that is not enough. We should not only watch over and protect the child but we should also seek to foster its development. And here the folk tale holds an incomparable position in the child's education. Let us think of the story of the *Star Money;* a little child, quite alone, goes out into the world. It gives all it has to beggar children and beggars, until at last in the dark cold night it has given away even its vest. And then comes its reward: silver coins rain from Heaven and even a little vest to cover its nakedness. Could anything be said more plainly — that one must risk all; risk all in love, and that Heaven will more than recompense one? Think also of the story, *The Water of Life.* The two elder, hardhearted brothers, who refuse to give the beggar any of their food, who wilfully destroy the antheaps, chase the fox and the ducks and separate them from their young — these two do not bring home the water of life. But the youngest son, who has pity for his fellow men and fellow creatures, he brings home the water of life. Could there be more profound stories, better suited to give the child courage to overcome all obstacles in the world and to find its way home? This deep apprehension of the significance of life lifts the folk tale above all other children's stories, which by comparison appear flat and meaningless. And here we return to Herder's words: "Even the belief in an *evil genius,* which travels with us, as if to spoil our best intentions — even this belief seems prejudicial to man's nobler nature."

(From *The Junior Bookshelf,* January 1961.)

CATHERINE STORR
Why Folk Tales and Fairy Stories live Forever

When *Where* asked me to write something about fairy and folk stories, based on a collection of what is currently published in this field, I was expecting perhaps 150 representational volumes. Instead of which I must have received over a thousand. I found myself knee-deep in fairy stories, hardly able to move about the house for folk tales. Since one must presume that publishers know their business, this number of newly published books on the market implies an equal, or nearly equal, demand. The interesting question, then, is Why? What have these stories got which warrants their longevity — their immortality?

And — another fascinating point — *what* is it that survives? Because if you compare different re-tellings of the same story, or different illustrations, it might seem as if this was not the same, but a new, story. The story, for instance, of the beautiful girl who marries an unknown, disguised or even invisible lover, who breaks her promise not to inquire into his real nature, and who then has to win him again through suffering, is familiar to us in the myth of Psyche and Eros. But how many of us recognise it again in the more familiar *Beauty and the Beast*? In *The Black Bull of Norroway*? In *East of the Sun and West of the Moon*?

Difference of custom, of country and of climate can alter any of these classic plots so that it is nearly, but not quite, unrecognisable. In this context I must record my delight in finding, in a collection of Ghanaian legends re-told by Peggy Appiah (Deutsch) the Ashanti version of *The Snow Maiden* in which the Pineapple Child, who gives the book its name, melts in the sun like her Northern sister, but is reduced not to snow water, but to oil.

Or take the innumerable re-tellings of *Snow White and the Seven Dwarfs*. It can be told deadpan, as originally by the brothers Grimm, with all the faceless cruelty at the end; or sweetly, sentimentally; at length; or briefly; making of it a romance or a comedy at will. If you were to see only the pictures with which all the different artists have decorated this one story, you'd hardly be able to perceive their common inspiration. And yet the tales, hacked about, cheapened, coarsened often both by words and pictures, do survive. In each new generation of children there are millions to whom these stories are as welcome and necessary as their daily bread. They must supply some very basic need. You could say that in the days when there were no fairy stories, it was necessary to invent them.

In an attempt to find some scholarly background for an inquiry into what this basic need is, I've been re-reading J.R. Tolkien's essay on fairy stories. He lists the four main qualities of the fairy story as Fantasy, Recovery (or a fresh sight of the too familiar), Escape and Consolation; and he thinks that these qualities are as desirable for adults as they are for children. Professor Tolkien is familiar with a wide range of sagas, fairy stories and myths, and has also shown in *The Lord of the Rings* that he is a true 'maker' or poet in the archaic sense of the word. But I think that he has, to a certain extent, fallen into a trap of which he is, nevertheless, aware.

"The analytical study of fairy stories is as bad a preparation for the enjoying or the writing of them as would be the historical study of the drama of all lands and times for the enjoyment or writing of stage-plays."

In spite of this, I find this essay, with its particularising of meanings — 'belief,' 'sub-creation,' 'fantasy and fancy,' 'fairy and faery' more analytical than inspiring.

I'm confirmed in my impression that the essence of these stories is something extremely difficult to define, even more difficult to convey effectively to someone else. Where, for me, Tolkien absolutely hits the nail on the head is right at the end of the essay, when he refers to the quality of 'joy.'

"It is the mark of a good fairy story . . . that . . . it can give to the child or the man who hears it, when the turn comes, a catch of the breath, a beat and lifting of the heart. . . . This joy . . . I have selected as the mark of the true fairy story. . ."

As Tolkien points out, this 'joy' is found in all sorts of other arts as well as in the art of the fairy and folk story; so I want to explore further to find out what else these stories contain which may explain their continuing appeal.

There is one element common to all of them, and this is the plot or story. In the best examples this not only has a most satisfactory beginning, middle and end; it also has that hallmark of a good plot, inevitability. The end is implicit in the beginning.

This is not to say that the end must always be the conventional one '. . . and they lived happily ever after.' Not at all; many stories end with loss, like the melting of the Snow Maiden I've already mentioned, the loss of the Seal wife, the death of the grandmother (and Red Riding Hood herself in some versions). But if the end is tragic, it is at the same time right, because the true fairy or folk story makes its own conventions and abides by them.

If the longing of the barren woman creates a child out of snow, then it is her business to guard that child against too fierce a light; if Psyche — or Pandora, or Bluebeard's wife or Eve — disobeys a precise prohibition, she must suffer. This inevitability — if you like this way of expressing the remorseless sequence of events in nature — is an essential ingredient in the 'true' fairy and folk story; it is also the one most commonly missing in the stories which are consciously invented.

Writers get carried away, particularly when they are already in the world of fantasy, by the power of creation, and they often produce what is not fantasy, but fantastick, trying to make up in gimmicks what is lost in urgency. For reasons which I shall come back to later, the 'true' fairy/folk tale has an element of harshness, of ruthlessness; and this points and implements the plot.

To children particularly these stories have an almost un-equalled capacity to arouse the question 'What happens next?' To stimulate this question is a vital part of the story-teller's art; it was on this that the itinerant ballad singers and narrators of epics and tales depended for their popularity; it was on this that Scheherazade counted to save the lives of her sister, herself and countless virgins to come. I know that today it is considered rather reprehensible for adults to admit to a taste for straight narrative; and 'unputdownable' is an adjective of praise only when it is applied to detective novels or, possibly, science fiction (even these are read apo-logetically, as it were). We really haven't progressed much since Jane Austen pointed out that the novel was undervalued.

Today, the anti-novel, in which plot is of no importance, is respectable, the 'story' is not. But the appetite for stories is still there, and there is an enormous attraction in the tale which engages one's attention immediately. Consider, to take three examples from widely different sources, the openings of the stories *Rumpelstilzen* (*Tom-Tit-Tot* in its English version), *Cinderella* and *Big Claus and Little Claus*. In each we are plunged at once into a situation full of dramatic possibilities – the miller's daughter who finds herself a Queen, set to an impossible task; the lovely, gentle girl oppressed by her step-mother and sisters: the sympathetic boasting of Little Claus which lands him in such trouble. We have to read on.

As we read we find ourselves caught up in what I think is the second, but equally important feature of this kind of literature; this is the opportunity it gives to most of us to identify with the principal characters. The themes of these stories are themes with which in our daydreams we are already familiar.

We have all imagined ourselves as the virtuous protagonist, triumphing over vice – *Snow White, The Wild Swans*; as out-witting something larger and stronger than ourselves – *The Gingerbread Man, The Gallant Little Tailor*; as attaining the recognition we deserve – *The Ugly Duckling, Cinderella*; as

succeeding where wiser men have failed — *The Golden Goose,
Mr Vinegar;* or, in a more romantic vein, as proving ourselves
by heroic deeds — the hero sagas, *The Golden Bird, The
Fairy of the Dawn,* and (on a more homely level) *Jack and
the Beanstalk.*

Taking these stories at their surface value only, for the
moment, they repeat to us, often with the added grandeur of
their setting, the stories we would like to believe about ourselves. We are the youngest sons who have no prospect of
winning the kingdom; we are the despised step-children (how
many of us fantasied in childhood that we were adopted?);
we are the small people who must learn to be clever before
we can compete with the strong; we are the outcasts who
will eventually receive homage; we are the generous-hearted
fools who in the end marry princesses.

I must disagree with Professor Tolkien's contention that
these stories are as much for adults as for children. I think
that the setting of the fairy story in the far past, in a country
where the laws of nature can be easily suspended or over-
ridden by magic, or where beasts talk and behave in the manner
of humans, is congenial to more children than adults. For
many children the atmosphere of marvels is no hindrance
to the belief, not that 'this might happen to me,' but that
'this is the sort of person I really am.' Adults in general need
their wish fulfilment fantasies spelled out in rather more
everyday language.

Readability. The implied promise of the granting of our
heart's desire. These two qualities belong to both folk and
fairy story, but the third is found almost exclusively in folk
tales, and this is humour. In high romance, and in the hero
legends, there is not so much scope for it. It might even be
dangerous to introduce it, since humour — I don't mean wit —
is apt to deflate a situation, to call into question values which
must be accepted for at least as long as the story lasts. (The
perfect example of this is Andersen's *The Emperor's New
Clothes.*) But folk stories are about ordinary people, peasants,
merchants, animals with human characteristics; and a common

feature of these stories is the downfall of dignity – the lion caught in a net, the miserly patriarch robbed, the out-witting of the mighty by the underdog.

Taken to an extreme, these become the nonsense stories, the tales of simpletons who win prizes by doing everything wrong; *Mr Vinegar,* the *Golden Goose, Hans in Luck.* Children, and adults, who find the more romantic stories too high-flown and remote from real life, are persuaded by the humour of some of the beast fables, especially when re-told in an up-to-date style as in Joel Chandler Harris's *Uncle Remus,* to forget the improbability of the tale and to enjoy the situation described. There are very few of us who are impervious to the comedy of seeing our betters brought down a peg and made to look ridiculous.

So far I've dealt with what the conscious mind appreciates in folk and fairy stories, but it wouldn't be right to pretend that – much as it is – this is all they have to offer. There are many stories which are compulsive reading the first time round, which have shape and elegance and humour, and which yet are never re-read. I believe that the enduring fairy stories have something beyond this, something more than immediately meets the eye.

This something is that they are concerned with the basic problems which we all share, but which are often buried deep in our unconscious minds, overlaid by the preoccupations of day to day life.

Let me illustrate what I mean. The reader, whether he be adult or child – does not think in psychologically analytical terms. He does not say to himself 'The story of the prince who has to kill a dragon and conquer the spell of the witch before he can win the princess and the kingdom, is the story of a young man who is initiated into manhood. He has to prove himself as strong as his father, the dragon, and as cunning as his mother, the witch, before he attains his identity as an adult; hence this story is important for me.' He doesn't say it in these words; but he feels the importance of the story nevertheless. He recognises it as something to do with his own experience.

And here, I think, is a good place to draw a clear distinction between folk and fairy stories, often as the boundaries must overlap. It seems to me that at this deeply unconscious level – what Freud called the 'latent content' when talking of dreams – folk stories deal with the problems of life at a fairly primitive level; with the need to fill one's own belly and not to become fodder for another's; with the need to keep warm and dry; to protect the young; and to keep ahead of one's neighbour. They are problems which man shares with other animals, which may be one reason why so many of these tales are expressed in terms of animal society. They are the problems connected with mere survival.

But the fairy stories are concerned with something else; the problem of identity. They are the stories of people who have to discover, each for himself, who they are, which may in part explain why so many of them open with a parent-child relationship – the old King with three sons, only one of whom can be the rightful heir; the royal pair with one daughter; the father whose new-born child threatens his own life; the magician's daughter; the widow's son.

Almost always there is conflict between parent and child or, more obviously, between step-parent and child. The Ugly Duckling is rejected by his putative mother as soon as he emerges from the egg. Cinderella is kept at work in the kitchen. Elsa's brothers are bewitched into the form of swans. Each eventually has to make good in his own right; that is to become the person he essentially is, to discard the character and shape imposed on him by others.

Of course these problems can be stated directly in psychological, in social, in moral, in ethical, in philosophical terms; but the strength of fairy and folk tales – and of novels, poetry and plays – is that they present the human predicament in the terms of character and plot (symbolically, is perhaps the right expression) so that while the conscious mind is employed in following the story, the unconscious is also being nourished.

And it is because this appeal is to the unconscious that it is so difficult to explain the satisfactoriness of the 'true' fairy story to someone who does not also feel it. It is, perhaps, partly what Professor Tolkien means when he writes of 'joy.' I'd call it also a feeling of recognition, but one which doesn't necessarily make it possible to say what has been recognised. We ask, sometimes, wanting to recall a name or a fact to another person's mind, 'Does it ring a bell?' And by listening to the reverberations of a private belfry, deep inside, to make out whether this note or that is a harmonic which can call out an answer from one of his silent bells, the person questioned is able to say whether or not the query has meaning for him. (One of my daughters, when younger, used joyfully to cry, 'It rings a very *strong* bell!' and I know exactly what she meant.)

The unconscious element in true fairy and folk stories not only makes it difficult to define their especial quality; it also makes forgeries in this line relatively easy to detect. They simply ring no bells. They are invented, on a purely conscious level. They may amuse, but they are apt to have only the trappings, the stock figures of the conventional fairy story, very little else.

In *The Magic Fishbone*, Dickens made the cardinal mistake of believing that the necessary ingredients of a fairy story were a family of King, Queen, princes and princesses, plus a fairy with magical gifts at her disposal. What he has produced is a tale of a middle-class family, archly told and with a repulsively moral streak. Thackeray's *Rose and the Ring* is a little less annoying because he at least doesn't preach and is a good deal more amusing, but it is nowhere near the real thing.

The fact that so many of the 'true' stories are set in palaces and deal with exalted people is not a mere bit of snobbery, it is essential to the meaning of the stories that the events recounted should be seen to be important. What happens to a peasant is important to him, but not necessarily to anyone else, but the fate of a King or of a prince will affect a whole kingdom. The king or prince becomes, thereby, the

71

representative of his people and so, to some extent, of mankind.

Of all the recent writers who have attempted to produce 'true' fairy stories, very few have realised this. Andersen did; he never made the mistake of depreciating the value of royalty; his princesses, whether good or bad, are never belittled. If they lose their dignity by letting themselves be kissed by swineherds, they lose the more by virtue of their position. Just as the fact that it is an Emperor who recognises the worth of the real – as opposed to the artificial – nightingale emphasises the importance of the distinction.

Another mark of the real thing, is, as I mentioned earlier, a quality which could, according to one's taste, be called 'realism' or 'ruthlessness'. By this I mean a refusal to escape into sentiment, or to side-step into another world, when the logical consequences of the action are unpleasant. A 'real' plot must follow up its issues to the end, whatever that may be, the death of the Queen (both the real and the step-mother of Snow White), the slaying of the Prince's faithful companion, or the second loss of Euridyce. To clap a happy ending, or the trivial explanation – 'It was all only a dream' – on to the end of a story which has hitherto taken itself seriously, is an artistic flaw almost never made by the tellers of those stories which have survived and been handed down to us and models of their kind.

To sum up, then, Fairy and folk stories tell us, in narrative form, of the great preoccupations of man's existence. They do this both in direct and in symbolic language. Picasso said, once, about Negro masks

"Men had made those masks and other objects for a sacred purpose, a magic purpose, as a kind of mediation between themselves and the unknown hostile forces that surrounded them, in order to overcome their fear and horror by giving it a form and an image."

One of the characteristics which seems to distinguish man from all other animals is this desire to impose a pattern on what mystifies and frightens him.

It is for this, I believe, that we should value these stories, for their beautiful form and for their message, if we can hear it. They speak in the language of poetry, and this is a language which cannot be faked. Either it springs from the heart — what D.H. Lawrence called 'the solar plexus' — or it is stillborn.

(From *Where*, 53, January 1971.)

PART TWO
Comics

INTRODUCTION

It is not usual to discuss comics in a book about children's literature, and I think this has often been a pity. Children read both, and in many ways one may complement the other. For the child, books can often represent adult choice, whether in Christmas present or school library, but once he gets pocket money, comics can be bought cheaply and are very much his own property. It should surprise no one to hear that children spend about three times as much of their pocket money on comics rather than on books. I have tried to suggest various reasons why this might be in the first extract, *Comics Today*, and I have also included another piece written by myself, *Anti-Superman*, which attempts to analyse one well-known comic character, again with the intention of asking why he has always been so popular with children.

In both articles I conclude that comics often have something quite valid to offer a young audience, but this is in their more positive aspects. Only an optimist could warm towards all areas of this field. Nicholas Johnson, for example, questions in the next extract the use and effect of crude stereotypes in comics when it comes to portraying foreigners. Since his article was written, comics have also been criticised for ignoring the fact that they now cater for a multi-racial audience in this country, many of whom may·look in vain in comic strips for any evidence that they exist at all. This is not a trivial point; it is grotesque for young coloured readers to be asked to identify with popular heroes who are always white. Research evidence suggests that this sort of distortion can help cause an upsetting loss of identity amongst black readers; it also does nothing to help young

77

white readers to prepare themselves for life in a multi-racial society themselves. Under pressure, publishers of comics insist that they have begun changes in these directions, but for all that, the social content of comics is worth keeping an eye on, along with other influences in the media on the growing child.

In fact, some control over comics has existed in this country since the *Children and Young Persons (Harmful Publications) Act*, 1955. This was brought in as a preventive measure against imported American horror comics. Such reading was often nasty and sadistic, and did not find many defenders, then or since. Although he is talking about pulp literature generally, J.B. Priestley's article, *The Real Clean-up*, is also a good description of the content of those early comics, and some of the questions they posed. The same type of argument can sometimes be heard now over best-selling sadistic paper-backs such as Richard Allen's *Skinhead* and *Suedehead*. What effects such literature might have, how teachers and parents should attempt to tackle it, are questions without easy answers. But if there was ever any feeling that the original Act banning horror comics in this country should be repealed, Angela Carter's *Once More into the Mangle*, the next extract, might make interesting reading. She writes about Japanese comics, finding very much the same flavour as early American horror comics, and whilst she does not find any marked bad effects, the over-all impression is ugly and depressing. At what stage does a safety valve become an irritant, or indeed responsible for the pressure it is then supposed to filter away? Are there any trends in our own comics in this direction? The 1955 Act has been little used, but this may not be to say that it has always been effective. Adult readers usually know little about contemporary comics — yet another type of underground literature — and looking at them can be interesting and sometimes revealing. For teachers in particular, comics can make good study material with a class — an area where pupils in many respects are bound to know more than those teaching them. I have tried to describe such techniques for discussing comics in my book, *Understanding the Mass Media.**

* Nicholas Tucker, *Understanding The Mass Media* (Cambridge University Press, 1966).

NICHOLAS TUCKER
Comics Today

Britain has always been a special place for comics. The first comic *ever* was produced here, either *Ali Sloper's Half-hour* in 1884, or *Comic Cuts* in 1890, according to definition. We still have more comics produced per head of child population than any other European country, and although accurate figures are impossible to come by, it would seem that about eight million comics are sold here every week now, and each copy read, on average, by about eight different children. In this way, almost every child still reads at least one comic a week, and many a good deal more.

These figures may surprise those who predicted a slump in comic reading with the coming of television. In fact, comics did suffer from this competition, but the 1950s saw a re-orientation of comics themselves, rather than any long-lasting decline of total sales. After all, children with TV to watch had far less time available, so the comic format had to alter in favour of the quick glance rather than the obsessive poring over close-packed columns of tiny print. In the same way, children began to have better libraries in and out of school, and more entertaining books to read. To counter these, comics had to re-emphasise their own, essentially strip-cartoon, technique, and in this process obviously the old 'text' comics with their adventure serials, such as *Rover* or *Champion*, suffered more than the 'funnies,' like the *Dandy* or *Beano*, which have never had any real equivalent in book form.

With the disappearance of comic loyalty at this time, many older publications found it difficult to make the change, and gradually comic production was merged into the hands of two companies that today practically dominate the whole comic scene: IPC and D. C. Thomson. Now market research on a large scale became the order of the day. When comics ceased to make a profit they were quickly dropped, which helps explain the bewildering series of changes seen in this market in the last two decades. No longer would old favourites be carried more or less for old time's sake, or because no one really knew how much money they were losing. But the life of many new comics has tended to be short too, however well the market has been researched beforehand. Perhaps children's tastes are changing quicker than before: how many TV series or pop stars manage to last over a single decade?

In many ways widespread television viewing, far from replacing comics, has simply taken over now as the chief target for parental wrath against the mass media. Comics are no longer accused, as they once were, of leading to poor eyesight because of their close print, or of causing faulty reading habits through not encouraging 'fluent left-right eye movements' by their substitution of speech bubbles for a written text. Instead, we hear now how television pictures can issue harmful radiation, lead to over-tiredness and even cause epileptic fits. The chief complaints about vulgarity and cruelty too are now directed almost solely against TV, especially since the 1955 Act banning the sale of horror comics.

In fact, modern research on comic reading points out several advantages children can gain, which may still be useful to pacify those very few parents who still see the comic as something to be exterminated (which nearly always means that it is driven underground instead). Where reading skills are concerned, some experiments by Neil Rackham of the Sheffield University Psychology Department suggest that comic strips offer an integrated visual aid to reading rather than a picture distraction from words in print.* Certainly the comic strip has been used most effectively in advertising, various forms of social propaganda campaigns, and even some textbooks; hardly fields where distraction from the essential text would be tolerated. As for the charge of luring children away from

* *Comics versus Education (New Education,* September, 1968).

81

serious reading, it has been suggested elsewhere that those children who read most comics are very often those who read most books too, showing a general liking for reading itself, rather than for any particular technique or publication.

Another charge, usually levelled against the American *Classics Illustrated* comics, which have some audience over here and may attempt anything from *Macbeth* to *Crime and Punishment* in multi-strip form, is that such things only serve to vulgarise great literature. But critics forget that it is just this type of popularisation – vulgar or not – which may possibly encourage some children from unbookish homes to try the real thing later on. Schools carry abbreviated versions of classics for the same reasons, but usually of such dullness that all interest is killed even at this primary stage. *Classics Illustrated* comics may be trivial, sometimes even ridiculous, but at least they are read and enjoyed and occasionally, in an essentially cinematic rather than literary way, even get quite close to the spirit of the original.

What about children who read nothing but comics? In this case it may be less relevant to blame the comic – or the child – than to investigate why this situation has arisen in the first place. Could it be that the child has very poor reading skills, or that the other books available to him are simply not very interesting or attractive? Or are the comics fulfilling some emotional need that is not being met elsewhere?

I should guess that most parents and teachers feel today that children's comics, on the whole, are fairly innocuous, to be dished out almost in contempt on wet weather days in school, or bought in quantity for a particularly arduous train journey. Their once-feared vulgarity can now be seen as part of their inspiration, as any visit to a pop art exhibition will testify.

Parents may be more worried by the amount of comics read than by any particular publication, and often try to lead their children on to higher things by buying them an educational comic (only 2% of educational comics, Neil Rackham estimates, are bought by children themselves).* These 'parent-

* *A Spoonful of Sugar (New Education,* November, 1968).

boys' differ in quality, and are almost certain to fail with the child if he is forced to read them. Many parents, writing in their comments to *Where*, report mixed responses in their own family, and some have abandoned educational comics in favour of giving the child money to buy books instead, or even opening a small account for him at a local bookshop. After all, Ladybird or Puffin books only cost a little more than some educational comics, which very rarely offer the same value for money, although the best of them are probably worth a look from time to time.

Would it be correct for most parents and teachers to write off the more popular comics as mere junk, only there, in the words of Jules Feiffer,* 'to entertain on the basest, most compromised of levels'? This could hardly explain the grip that comics can get upon children at certain ages, involving a depth of concentration that can make them quite oblivious to friends, parents and teachers − sometimes at their peril. As Havelock Ellis wrote in his *Autobiography*, the effect of his early reading of *The Marvel*, a forerunner to later horror comics, was 'A kind of fever . . . an excitement which over-whelmed all ordinary considerations.'

Perhaps one reason for this sort of situation is that real comics, as opposed to 'parent-buys' like the bulk of infant and educational comics, are aimed directly at the child, to be bought by him with his own pocket money and without adult prompting or supervision. The sense of ownership, therefore, is complete: the comic is yours to swap, store or discard entirely, as you wish. And although playground conversation these days may be less about this week's comics than last night's TV, comic readership is still one of the ways a child can initiate himself into a world of knowledge and experience shared only by his contemporaries. As well as this social side to comic reading, of course, the material within them will also cover some of the individual child's most basic fantasies, so often ignored by his other, more respectable literature.

For example, comics aimed at the junior market − known

* Jules Feiffer, *The Great Comic Book Heroes* (Allen Lane 1970).

otherwise as the 'thick-ear trade' — are full of stories about temper tantrums, oral gratification (those tremendous iced cakes and cow pies!) messy play, and of course frequent and prolonged violence against persons and property. In their way, these recurrent themes echo infantile moods and fantasies that an older child is gradually growing away from, but may like the opportunity to re-visit in the safety of comic reading.

Elsewhere, the comic figures depicted in 'the funnies' tend to be ugly, lazy, badly dressed and greedy, usually living in gritty urban surroundings — once more, for the child, a welcome balance to the idealised characters that crop up in so much of the more conventional literature for children, and in particular those books that are used for teaching reading. Indeed, among all the literature available to the child, comics are sometimes the only publications that really acknowledge the violent, uncivilised aspect of his environment and personality, without necessarily inflaming it. Rather, violence in this sense tends to be neutralised and contained by humour, plus an old comic tradition that practically always shows authority winning in the end — whatever sort of upsets have happened just before.

Different types of fantasies, of course, are fulfilled in comics for older children, who are at the stage of preferring adventure stories to knockabout fun. Archetypal plots built on common human daydreams, such as those contained in *Jack the Giant-Killer, Cinderella,* or *Aladdin and his Lamp,* will turn up in different guises, whether in stories about football sides, boarding schools or the Wild West. Children who are at the age of scorning fairy stories can still allow themselves, without any loss of face, to read about Superman and his magical powers. There is also in some of these comics that special, almost surrealist strain, especially appealing to the sense of humour and imagination of a child, who is always ready to suspend disbelief at a moment's notice. Where else but in a comic, for example could there be a story called *The Hungry Head*, about a fat but charming headmistress who goes in for pie-eating competitions in disguise?

Where else, again, could any author begin a story with an
introduction as outrageously cool as: ' "Well, I think that's
the end of a very, interesting lesson," said Mr. Brown, the
school teacher who had had the misfortune to change into
a walrus after taking a Magic Wishing Pill.'

Perhaps the great age for reading comics, certainly for a
boy, is already over by the time he reaches secondary school,
ready to assume grown-up values, and no longer so willing to
identify in the perpetual battle in comics between the little
and the big. Some boys may go on to those comics issued in
booklet form, usually about war and cowboys, and there are
also some American comics for this age group, but on the
whole sales in this particular field are not very high.

Girls present a different picture: there is much more of a
continuum between their junior comics, where they fall in
love with ponies, to their teenage comics where they shift
their attention to young men and pop stars, while making
frequent use of the Readers' Advice columns, a constant
feature of these papers, on their problems in this direction.
Later on, without the need for very much readjustment, many
of them will move on to women's magazines.

There is no such direct line of development for boys, however, who may go on to read anything in adolescence from
those multifarious technical magazines to poor imitations of
Playboy, or those other rather depressing publications special-
ising in a stereotyped brand of mildly pornographic violence.
(It is interesting, though, that at the same time as all this,
many adolescent boys will also read their sister's love comics,
although at home rather than in public.)

But most English comics are aimed almost exclusively at
primary school age children, which means that they have to
be cheap, and thus rather limited at the same time. Unlike the
best children's books, there is little to interest the parent in
his children's comics, except perhaps nostalgia for those very
few that have survived since his childhood. The artistry tends
to be crude, with very few of those exciting cinematic effects
and witty, energetic dialogue that runs through some French

and American comic strips. Indeed, the widely syndicated comic strip artist in other countries is often a well-known figure, signing his own strip each time and employing a proper studio which, in the case of Hergé's *Adventures of Tintin*, may amount to different individuals looking after script, colouring, landscapes and speech balloons.

English comics, on the other hand, work almost entirely by commission. Stories are farmed out, often to artists abroad, and the result tends to be workable but anonymous and unexciting: a perpetual seat in the stalls watching antics running along very well-worn lines of plot and stylised dialogue.

Perhaps the most important role of comics in this country has been to act as a common bond to the vast union of children, by dealing with matters that amuse and intrigue them at a price they can afford. An imagination dominated, and therefore limited, by comics would be a poor one. But in a supporting role, as it were, comics have their place in childhood which it would be difficult to deny or displace. At their best, which must be the child's rather than the adult's judgement, comics can occupy a very favourite space for some time in a child's life, and however much comics have been attacked in the past, most critics have generally admitted a soft spot for those they read when they were young – when things were quite different, of course!

(From *Where*, 47, January 1970.)

Anti-Superman

Today, and for a good many years previously, I should guess
that the best known and most popular literary figure with the
bulk of primary school children is that great baroque
character Desperate Dan, now in his thirtieth uninterrupted
year and still taking up his full page in the *Dandy*, which remains, with its twin the *Beano*, the most widely-read comic
in this country. He still lives in Cactusville, a timeless place
set in the American West where people have Abe Lincoln
beards and cowboy hats, but are ruled by a mayor with the
help of English policemen and occasionally play the odd
game of cricket.

Desperate Dan himself is a domesticated cowboy living
quietly with his Aunt Aggie, whom he respects and obeys,
and although he began in 1937 as a bad-tempered "heavy",
hence his original name, he has long since settled into an
amiable if rather bovine good humour. His chief problem,
and at the same time his greatest asset, is his enormous,
god-like strength. Inadvertently pulling down buildings, im-
provising bridges out of iron girders, or quite literally moving
mountains, Desperate Dan can only be described as a natural
force, rather like some of the heroes to be found in ballads
or fairy stories. When he peels onions, his tears create rivers to
cultivate the crops; the bristles on his chin or elsewhere are
often put to versatile use ("Your hairy chest makes a swell
saw, Dan"); he can score by blowing the football from one
goal to the other, and he has many other fairly earthy
functions ("Dan's sweating so hard that the sweat is carrying
the logs to the river"). Always hopeful, Dan is often given
jobs whose prospects he usually wrecks by sneezing too hard

and breaking every window, or by accidentally walking through a wall, but although his fellow citizens often end up by jumping in the air or falling in a dead faint to express their rage or surprise, they seldom punish him for this almost inevitable destruction. Indeed, he is often rewarded for his more useful acts, such as tying thieves in knots, stopping runaway trains or holding together broken dams.

In this way, of course, Dan is an anti-Superman, performing some of the same feats but laughably and without the vainglory or earnest moralizing. He too has a uniform, not of billowing cloak and blazoned tunic, but in fact the clothes he always wears; a tiny white hat with a black brim, unless he is in bed where he has the full nightshirt and hat to match, neckscarf, a white shirt with rigid protruding buttons, a horribly shrunken black waistcoat encasing his enormous and permanently inflated chest, a holster containing a pistol never to my knowledge put to any use, knee breeches and leather boots with spur attachment. His most prominent feature is his enormous Habsburg chin, always covered by dotted black bristles which he has been known to pluck and use as steel darts. With all this, Desperate Dan is quite extraordinarily ugly.

This very ugliness, however, may be an important clue to Dan's popularity with children. They know and sometimes relish the fact that they too can be rough, coarse and ugly at times, and undoubtedly get rather tired of the handsome well-mannered Dream Children that still so often turn up in the books their parents or teachers tend to suggest for them. And if children like to deal with their own sometimes frightening fantasies of aggression or omnipotence by externalizing them romantically with Superman, they can also do the same by externalizing them ridiculously with Desperate Dan. For Dan can be very violent at times, and like the early Walt Disney a lot of this is cheerfully directed against animals ("Gosh. Dan's hauled the elephant's tail and pulled its trunk in!"). But even here, Dan's superhuman onslaughts are funny, not frightening, involving a safe violence that does not seem to do any irrevocable or painful harm. He is never deliberately nasty or anti-social; indeed, he spends a lot of his time trying to control his equally prognathic but naturally troublesome nephew and niece, very often with a sound spanking.

There are, of course, many other reasons for Dan's popularity. The story and characters are almost obsessionally repetitive, with some rigid conventions: the schoolmaster must always carry his mortar board and cane, the mayor his chain of office and the thief his mask and bag of loot. The language is easy to read if occasionally eccentric: "Suffering Snakes", "Jumping Cats" or just "Aw Shucks" are some of Dan's favourite exclamations. There are enormous and frequent meals usually consisting of "Cow Pie", and this means exactly what it says, head, horns and tail included. This sort of oral gratification fantasy, provided for by endless pictures of cakes, sweets and ice-cream in most comic strips for the young, here seems to reach an extreme point. There is also a lot of what infant teachers call messy play, involving paint, ink or mud very often spurting up into people's faces leaving visible only a pair of outraged eyes. The tone is always strictly child-centred, and Dan himself often plays with the Cactusville children. During the last war some effort was made to bring in adult politics ("I am Herr Hitler. I would become der emperor of the world. You are der cowboy you would become der emperor of the cows"). But obviously readers preferred the atmosphere of the Mid-West somewhere around the introduction of the first Ford car, and Hitler was withdrawn to his own comic strip: "Addie and Hermy, the Nasty Nazis".

But it is obviously Dan's great mock-heroic strength that is the chief gimmick in these comic strips. Faced with exploiting this absurd force week after week, Dan's authors soon exhausted their more rational store of ideas, and thus perhaps unintentionally were forced back upon a type of zany surrealist humour always highly delightful to children, whether it be in Edward Lear, "Hey Diddle Diddle, the Cat and the Fiddle", or in the child's own vivid and very often bizarre imagination itself. Established children's writers, with one eye perhaps upon the parents, often seem too self-conscious to slip into this vein really easily. But in the *Dandy* Desperate Dan will actually lift and walk underneath a complete river bed, smack a recalcitrant camel so hard that its hump comes out on the bottom side, or when meeting a Red Indian offer to play cowboys and Indians. Dr. Frederick Wertham in his book *Seduction of the Innocent* deplores comics that give children the wrong ideas about physical laws, as in pictures where Superman is seen lifting up a building while he himself is not standing on the ground, or stopping an aeroplane when both he and it are in mid-flight. Desperate Dan breaks many more laws than this and far more casually; like children's imagination itself, there is virtually no limit to what he is going to think of next.

Another good example of the endless variations on a gimmick leading to something like the Theatre of the Absurd can be found in the almost equally famous but now deceased Keyhole Kate, with Korky the cat the only survivor until just recently of the old prewar *Dandy*, and a devoted eavesdropper and voyeur. It is not surprising that many children, full of their own fantasies and curiosity about what adults do when they are behind closed doors and by themselves, should feel a mixture of interest and amused contempt for this unpleasant little spy. She too is fearfully ugly, with plaits, glasses, a long, thin nose often inflamed or wrapped around in a bandage as a result of injuries sustained while looking through keyholes, a short gym slip and antennae-like legs clothed in black stockings. When all the other characters in her strip try to baulk her by looking through their own keyholes first, Kate accepts the scene as normal, merely commenting "Bah! They're all booked today". Her chief enemy, Cousin Cuthbert, teases her by showering cut-out paper keyholes from an upstairs window, and this time Kate is surprised, producing an almost poetic line: "It's snowing keyholes". Another time she sees an exceptionally large keyhole: "Coo! — What a beauty!" When one of her victims actually opens the door and says "There, now you can see inside ever so much better", one is hardly surprised when Kate slams the door again and continues as before. The fact is, of course, that Kate is obsessed with orifices almost for themselves, let alone what one can see through them, even stopping for a hole in the road that happens to look like a keyhole. Like many of her readers, Kate is clearly going through what psychoanalysts refer to as the anal stage of child development.

Keyhole Kate regularly receives the almost ritualistic punishment reserved for naughty children in the last picture of the strip, either by being kicked in the pants, hit with walking sticks, or even more serious accidents which may involve her being carried out on a stretcher by laughing ambulance men. She is that pariah among children, the tell-tale and the sneak, but even if her weekly punishment is popular, most children probably get some vicarious satisfaction too from watching Kate fearlessly nosing her way through the same forbidden openings and discovering secrets every week. Once again, by rendering their own fantasies ridiculous, she may have helped some of her audience come to terms with them.

The fact that the *Dandy* and *Beano* have remained afloat while so many competitors have sunk suggests that they are both particularly aware, at an intuitive as well as at a conscious level, of what children want and like. In this, perhaps, they are genuine children's newspapers: inexpensive, freely available in newsagents' shops, and written not with paragraphs but with pictures so that almost any child can get something out of them. In these comics authority figures, such as teachers. Dad or anyone else who is big and a potential threat to those who are little, are savagely satirized, although unless they are mere bullies who need to be taught their weekly lesson, they are often allowed to win in the end to face the anarchy of the little people on the next occasion.

These adventures and characters are still discussed and imitated in school playgrounds along with popular television programmes, just as adults often find a common bond in discussing the latest news, and many children will store these comics and reread them innumerable times, often after they have gone to bed. In my experience, it is rare to see a child actually laughing out loud when reading comics; more often they seem to be treated with intense concentration. We can only guess what is going on in the child's mind, but the continuing popularity, for example, of Desperate Dan and Keyhole Kate over the years may be due in some measure to their authors having stumbled upon a story-line which catered in a minor way for certain childhood tensions and fantasies in the course of entertaining its audience with some of the rough energy, crude wit and fertile imagination of an older tradition. A child who reads nothing but comics, of course, is getting a highly inadequate diet, but experience and research seem to suggest that there is nothing educationally or psychologically wrong with a mixed diet of books and some comics — except for the anxiety it still gives rise to among some teachers and parents.

(From *The Times Literary Supplement*, June 6, 1968.)

NICHOLAS JOHNSON
What do Children learn from War Comics?

The objects of this article are to consider the presentation of
nationality in one of the mass media available to young
children — the comics — and to present evidence on some of
the probable effects of reading war comics. The content of
comics has been studied before, most strikingly perhaps by
Orwell in his article on "Boys' Papers," written in 1939, and
by Wertham in his book on crime and horror comics *Seduction of the Innocent* which was published in 1955. Both these
authors were convinced that children were affected by reading
comics, but both were prevented by the nature of their
inquiry from obtaining empirical evidence of this supposed
influence on the normal child (although Wertham does use
case material from the clinical study of disturbed children in
his book).

Orwell's main case was that the 1910 world view he saw
the boys' papers as presenting in 1939 must have helped
preserve the reactionary society supported by the press lords.
The fact that the comics were inspired by an outdated and
conservative ideology was, he claimed, "Only unimportant if
one believes that what is read in childhood leaves nothing
behind."

Wertham described the effect of the particularly brutal and
perverted horror comics he studied as the "psychological
erosion of children."

But, in opposition to these views, there are more moderate
voices extolling the resistance of the child's mind to violence
or propaganda. A recent article in *The Guardian* which reviewed the presentation of foreigners in boys' comics dramati-
cally raised the question of the effects of such presentation,

93

but contained the following reassurance: "An educational psychologist on the staff of Manchester education committee does not think that children are influenced to any great extent by seeing all Germans, Italians and Japanese as jokers or knaves." The author of the article feels his anonymous psychologist might not be so sanguine about the effect of American war comics, but is not able to present evidence which would allow us to make some relative evaluation of the alarmist and quietist positions. Later in this paper, some evidence will be given which bears upon this point.

Before examining the content of some children's comics and their possible effects on their readers, it is reasonable to ask whether children of between seven and eleven really have any concepts of or opinions about other countries. Evidence from other studies we have conducted suggest that they do, at least on the emotional side: that is to say that one of the first things a child learns about countries is that some of them, most noticeably his own, are good, while others are bad. While it is not possible to say that he learns this before he has acquired *any* factual information, his information is so minimal as to make it extremely unlikely that his likes and dislikes are based upon it. The agreement between groups of children about the relative pleasantness or unpleasantness of countries is, however, very considerable: for example, the group mean preference ranks of ten prominent countries obtained from two separate samples of 60 Oxford primary schoolchildren were correlated at +0.97.

How is it that primary schoolchildren have come to agree about the relative merits of various countries? Who tells them that England, Australia, America and France are to be liked, while Russia, Japan, China, Germany and India are to be disliked? The answer must lie largely in what parents, teachers and other adults tell the children, and, of course, this source is a difficult one to investigate. When we turn to the mass media, however, it becomes possible to analyse the content of the material presented, and to evaluate the effect of the media by comparing children exposed to it with those who are not.

Himmelweit *et al*, in their study *Television and the Child*, took care to provide a control group against which to evaluate the effects of a year's viewing on the children under study. Their findings as related to the presentation of nationality on television were that children who watched it tended to become more objective about, and less prejudiced towards, foreign countries and foreigners. They also state that the children's opinions about other nationalities tended to come more into line with the way these nationalities were presented in television programmes. In general, their finding was that children did tend to be affected by the programmes but that, as the BBC provided balanced and unprejudiced material, the influence tended to be for the better. A recent study conducted in America, however, claimed to trace a definite effect of televised films in leading children to develop conceptions of international relations appropriate to the 1940s but "dangerously inadequate" in the 1960s.

Let us now turn to the comics. While children do not spend as much time reading comics as watching television, the time they do spend on them is likely to be considerable. The children interviewed in our sample estimated that they read, on average, over two comics a week. While circulation figures are not published for all the major comics, those which do exist allow us to judge what a large market these publications, often unnoticed by adults, must have. For example, *Robin, Wham, TV Comic, Lion, Princess, Valentine* and *Look and Learn* each comfortably outsell the *New Statesman, The Spectator* and *The Listener* combined.

The sample of comics of which we have made a partial content analysis consists of three consecutive weeks' issues of 40 weekly comics and children's periodicals available in Oxford. Most of the titles listed in table 1 are produced, as in Orwell's day, by Fleetway Publications or D. C. Thomson, although very few of the present titles have been in existence for more than ten years. In addition to these comics, a set of eight British and four American war comics, which are more sporadic in their appearance in newsagents in Oxford, was examined.

A cursory examination of these comics shows that they are a powerful source of nationality references, but suggests that a more careful analysis needs to be made in order to separate the different ways in which other countries and people from them are introduced. One of the most striking of these is through the depiction of real and imaginary wars, which appears to enable the producers of comics to introduce violence and death of a more-or-less sanctioned kind. As will be seen, it is also the occasion for the introduction of "name-calling," the use of generally pejorative labels to describe the enemy.

Not all comics, of course, concern themselves with war, and the range of publications named by the children as comics contains a great variety of material.

BASIC DATA ON COMICS AND THEIR READERSHIP IN A PRIMARY SCHOOL SAMPLE

group	titles	mean nationality references per issue	mean international killings or near killings	readership: sometimes or regularly boys	girls
		no.	no.	%	%
nursery	Bimbo, Jack & Jill, Playhour, Robin, Teddy Bear	1.2	–	30	67
juvenile	Beano, Beezer, Buster, Dandy, Smash, Sparky, Topper, Wham	8.1	1.0	93	70
television	Huckleberry Hound, Lady Penelope, TV Comic, TV 21	5.9	0.2	77	70
boys'	Champion, Eagle, Hornet, Lion, Ranger, Tiger, Valiant, Victor	45.9	7.5	90	17
girls'	Brownie, Bunty, Diana, Judy, June, Princess	22.0	0.3	–	70
romantic/ teenage	Mirabelle, Petticoat Trend, Valentine	31.4	0.3	–	7
educational	Finding out, Look & Learn, New Knowledge, Treasure, Wonderland	68.7	0.6	3	–
war GB: US:	Air Ace Picture Library Battle Picture Library Commando, War Picture Library Army War Heroes Fightin' Air Force Fightin' 5 Navy War Heroes	60.3	18.6	67	13

It was therefore decided to classify the titles examined on the basis of the type of material they presented; the headings used in the table are based upon this classification.

The first three groups of comics show a development in theme from the totally familiar to the totally fantastic. In the Nursery group, for children who have just learnt to read, we find the comfortable world of home and school. The central character is a child or, commonly, a child-substitute — an animal in the reassuring possession of entirely human characteristics. When we look at Juvenile comics, our horizons expand and the variety of themes increases greatly. The child heroes now frequently possess special powers, shrinking fluids, robot friends or magic toys, all of which introduce some fantastic distortion into an otherwise familiar world. Some adult heroes are found, mainly in space sagas or the occasional war story. When war is depicted it usually involves laughable armies or child heroes, and rather little violence.

The use of adult heroes becomes more common in the Television group of comics, whose stories are largely based on popular television series. The dominating themes are of international or intergalactic agents, spies and criminal organisations locked in eternal, but basically non-ideological, conflict. Gadgets, robots and machines are everywhere, and the puppet heroes of children's television are often central characters. This is a world of mechanical super-fantasy: a surrogate TV, looking out upon the adult fantasy-worlds of space, James Bond and science fiction. References to nationality are not common, and certainly no nationality is singled out as an enemy.

As we turn to comics for adolescent readers, fantasy becomes tempered by realism, and flesh-and blood heroes in more normal surroundings are found. Boys' comics concentrate most on war and sport, although there are remnants of the more juvenile fantasy themes. Nationality is prominently referred to in this popular group and, as will be seen from the table, violence and killing are quite common. Girls' comics also present a version of the real world: one of careers, girls making their own way, school and animals. Foreign countries provide exotic settings for adventure, as they do in the Romantic and Teenage group of publications. Here we find the familiar teenage world of romance, appearance, pop records, television and films. This is a less diversified world than that of the Girls' group, and it is interesting to speculate why.

The Educational group contains publications intended for both young and older children: they share the intention, however, of presenting a picture of the world as it really is. The most common objects of interest are animals, history, literature and technology. Notice that while nationality is frequently referred to in this group, the proportion of violent references to nationality is low. In the War comic group, however, it is very high, these comics being quite single-mindedly concerned with the presentation of war material. It is also interesting to compare our sample's readership of the Educational and War groups.

On the basis of the analysis presented in the table, and a general consideration of the themes used by these comics, it was felt that those comics most likely to provide a source of emotive attitudes to other nations were those which frequently presented the highly charged themes of war and international violence. Let us see how war is presented when it occurs, for the style of presentation, as well as the sheer quantity of war references, serves to distinguish the groups of comics listed above. As war references hardly ever occur in Nursery, Television, or Romantic and Teenage comics, these will be ignored in the following comparison.

The Second World War, with which nearly all war stories are concerned, has suffered a subtle distortion in its translation to the comic books. Those on the "wrong" side have been reduced to Germany and Japan, with Italy very rarely appearing except as a battle setting, while Britain's allies are all white and English speaking: America, Australia, and New Zealand, with the French appearing in the occasional supporting role.

When war references occur in Juvenile comics, they are

often to joke forces (for example, General Nitt and his Barmy Army) and characters such as Corporal Clott who never become involved in operations of a truly military nature. There are, however, occasional stories which introduce genuine conflict against the Japanese or the Germans. A serial entitled "The Mighty Misfits" in *Buster* includes a most interesting character, Albert "Bomber" Briggs, and his diminutive ally Socrates Smith. Briggs is allowed the comic licence of extreme language, calls the Japanese "Japs" or "Yellow Chops," the Germans "Jerries" or "Nazis," but is basically a comic character whose violence is described on the level of the "good scrap" and rarely leads obviously to death or serious injury. Similarly, Rusty Rae, a British hero disguised as a Burmese elephant boy (and raising the interesting question of why a real Burmese could not have been used instead) fights the Japanese, using impromptu tactics such as the firing of hornets nests into their ranks or charging them on the back of his elephant. The few war themes that are developed in this Juvenile group of comics are essentially in accordance with the philosophy, implied by Orwell, of teaching the rather comic foreigner a British lesson.

When we move on to the portrayal of war in the Boys' group of comics, we find a great increase in the frequency of war themes and increasing realism in the depiction of the violence of war. Some comic characters are retained. Captain Hurricane and Maggot Malone of the *Valiant* for example, being similar in type to Bomber Briggs and Socrates Smith of the Juvenile group. Captain Hurricane also uses "comic" language as he sets about his enemies: he calls the Japanese, for example, "Little Yellow Monkeys" and "Rice-eating Rats." The author does not, doubtless, intend us to take this too seriously as Hurricane is in one of his "ragin' furies." Other somewhat unrealistic types of character to appear in this group are "The Jailbird Commandoes," released from prison to fight the Germans, and "The Amazing Jack Wonder": "an overdose of a fantastic drug had given Jack the power to change himself into almost anything he wishes." Needless to

99

say Jack employs his remarkable talents in the service of the Allies.

In the main, however, the many war stories in this Boys' group of comics are straightforward accounts of fighting in almost every theatre of operations of the Second World War, as well as one story dealing with the Northwest Frontier. The British forces, of course, win almost every engagement. The only concession in the presentation of war to the tender age of the readership is in an avoidance of much actual blood or maiming: injury and death usually occur at a distance, and our forces do not use flame throwers or nuclear weapons.

The inclusion of war themes in the Girls' comics is very rare, the only story exclusively concerned with this theme in the group being "War Nurse Vicki" in *Bunty*. It is similar in its general presentation to that of the Boys' comics, but, of course, deals with tending the wounded rather than the actual prosecution of the war.

In the Educational comics written for older children, war themes seem neither to be avoided nor to be especially sought out. Descriptions of historic battles and of wars in general emerge from these magazines' conscientious historical articles which are most concerned with Britain, Europe and the English-speaking world.

The realistic portrayal of war is the exclusive preoccupation of the War comics. The British War comics considered consist of a complete picture story which takes up the whole issue and which usually strongly emphasises the role of one of the three services. The heroes are usually British, but sometimes include Australians and New Zealanders. The enemy is either German or Japanese. Reference is sometimes made to allies, particularly the Americans who are not always presented in an unequivocally favourable light. Italy, France and Belgium are generally presented as locales rather than in any sense as nations actually involved in the fighting.

One of the most characteristic differences from the Boys' comics is found in the emergence of some kind of personality for the central characters other than a complete stereotype.

The story often revolves around a feared failing of character, often one that has been exposed early in the war, and the subsequent vindication of the hero when his "real" bravery is shown. Language we might think amusing from Captain Hurricane becomes serious in the realistic war context presented by this kind of comic. The enemy is described, either by the comic itself or by British characters, as "deadly and fanatical; lousy stinking rats; brainless scum; swine; devils; filthy dogs; slippery as snakes; or slit-eyed killers." A sample of the frightening propositions lightly put forward should include "these Japs aren't human beings," and "the only good Germans are dead ones."

Not to be outdone, the enemy also shout, rant and scream: "Feuer — destroy the Englander Schwein-hunds; death to the British; banzai; the white dogs bar our path; we are here to fight for our Fuehrer, not play nursemaid to squealing casualties." Faced with this kind of thing, one Australian hero "didn't much fancy the idea of his country being overrun by yellow men." The British and their allies are forced to retaliate, and they are thorough about it. They "hose the Nazis with slugs" and "give them a bellyful o' lead." All the while, however, they retain their typically British characteristics of boyishness, courage, valiance and cool daring. All this is accompanied by many pictures of probable and certain death in greater or lesser detail.

The American war comics examined show certain points of difference from the British ones already described. They have several stories in each issue and, although the Second World War is still the major theme, they do not seem quite so whole-hearted about it as their British counterparts. In addition, they present political references, especially to the communists, as a sub-dominant theme. We find here reference to wars other than the Second World War, in particular the Korean war, and the names Communists, Commie and Red appear, on average, 8.8 times per issue. It is only in the American War comics that one comes across, for example, "so we cured Commie neighbours of their dirty

101

little habits," or "Moscow's puppets, always ready to pounce when we show a sign of weakness."

While the Japs can, in these comics, still come "silently out of the jungle, screaming hideously at the last moment," there are signs of a desire to shift the focus to the present (which does not exist in the British War comics). The East Germans appear as a particularly convenient enemy possessing simultaneously the hate-potential of both Nazis and Communists. There are even some attempts to make the idea of nuclear war familiar and acceptable: "In the future, there is a great possibility that most of the operations will be of the push-button type." So, although the most frequent concern is still with the Second World War, pictured here as America (virtually unaided) versus Germany and Japan, there are signs that the American war comic is more and more tending to present its own distorted view of the present and future as well.

One of the most striking things about the way war is treated in those comics in which it occurs, is that it is *not* used to show the virtues of international solidarity. One might think that, if war is suitable material for children at all, it should be a war which does more to encourage notions of comradeship and alliance.

The most obvious distinction to be made between the groups of comics examined is between those employing war as a major theme (Boys' and War) and the rest. The Boys' and War comics involve a higher rate of reference to nationality than any of the other comic groups except Educational, and in addition, as inspection of table 1 will show, a high proportion of these nationality references is associated with scenes of killing and violence.

(From *New Society,* July 7th, 1966 — an abridged version of the original article in which evidence is presented suggesting that children who read boys' and war comics acquire attitudes to nations which correspond to the alliances of the Second World War. Details of this and related research will also be found in Dr. N.B. Johnson's Ph.D. thesis available through the University of London Library.)

J. B. PRIESTLEY
The Real Clean-up

Being greedy and self-indulgent, I often eat too much, and I smoke too much strong tobacco, with the result that I sleep badly. This means that I do a great deal of reading in bed. Literature and books that have ideas in them are no use to me as bed books because they excite me and make me more wakeful than ever. So I read a great many detective stories and thrillers of the better sort, most of which I borrow from our local bookshop library. Many of these, by writers unknown to me, I glance at and then throw aside, because they cannot be read even in the small hours. But this means that I take a dip into all manner of stuff, and do at least learn what is being written, published, and read.

It has been said that those of us who read fiction of this kind are secretly attracted to it by the violence it depicts. This in my own case, I most stoutly deny. What attracts me to it, simply as bed reading, is that it offers me narrative on a certain artificial level, not unlike the *Arabian Nights*. I like narrative — and am no bad hand at it myself — and if it is free from challenging ideas and the oppressive but fascinating thickness of something like real life, then I skim along easily, with part of my mind sufficiently engrossed while the remainder of it prepares itself for sleep. A certain amount of violence is almost inevitable in stories that deal with crime and its detection, though I have long held that there is too much murder in such fiction, too many corpses and not sufficient ingenuity in offering us riddles not stained with blood. (For example, we are told that every year hundreds of people simply disappear. What stories could be told about them!) And, it must be remembered, some of our best

103

novelists both here and in America are fascinated by violence: this is, after all, an age of violence. But as a reader – and certainly as a reader-in-bed – I am not attracted by it; and indeed most of the stories I throw aside sicken me because they describe, with a gusto missing from the rest of their narratives, scenes that descend to the depths of atrocity. Moreover, they ask not only for our interest but for our admiration. It is not just the villains who smash noses, gouge eyes, and beat people to a jelly; the heroes do it too, and indeed are handier at it than the villains. There is a familiar type of husky private detective who is better at getting results than the police are, just because he behaves like a member of the Gestapo or the S.S. And now, I am sorry to say, there seem to be even more of these tough guys in English than in American fiction.

This is not a good dream life to offer adolescent lads. Much of this fiction is of course aimed at them. The hero is what they would like to be. Outwardly he is everything they are not: tall, broad-shouldered, very strong, very brave, attractive to the girls; he is "a snappy dresser," negligently drives a very fast car, drinks all manner of exotic stuff (he hardly ever eats), and strolls in and out of strange night clubs, throwing pound notes about, not giving a damn for anybody except the enchanting blonde in the corner. And if you are seventeen, five foot four and rather puny, a victim of acne, with only two shabby suits, a job in a cheese warehouse, no entranced girls, two and eightpence to last you until Friday, and several jeering brothers and sisters, then you want to live gloriously, if vicariously, with such a hero. Nothing new here: boys and youths have been identifying themselves with the Hero for thousands of years; this cannot be stopped. But we might see to it that the Hero is not so often kicking people in the stomach and then smashing their faces into red pulp. We do not want to find ourselves surrounded on a dark night by youths whose imaginations have been nourished on such scenes. It will be as well if the citizens of tomorrow do not take it for granted that people they dislike should be beaten, pounded, minced. The red-pulp view of life should be discouraged.

If some of our cleaners-up would stop thinking about sex and take a look at this violent cruel stuff, they might yet do us a service. This is not likely to happen. It is the pleasures of sex and not the pains of cruelty that start the puritan crusading.

. . . Nine youngsters out of ten will sooner or later discover sex for themselves, even if their favourite hero is not always being voluptuously entangled. But this cruel violence is something else. It is by no means an essential part of us. No doubt there is in us the germ of it, a spark of savagery, especially in youth. One of the aims of civilisation is to smother that spark, to provide an environment in which that germ cannot flourish and multiply. But here in this popular fiction the whole civilised trend is being carefully reversed. It is more than a question of manners. There is much of our early fiction — in Fielding and Smollett, for example — a lot of rough-and-tumble, knockabout brutality, as much a reflection of its time as Hogarth's pictures were. But this new violence, with its sadistic overtones, is quite different. It is not simply coarse, brutal from a want of refinement and nerves, but genuinely corrupt, fundamentally unhealthy and evil. It does not suggest the fairground, the cattle market, the boxing booth, the horseplay of exuberant young males. It smells of concentration camps and the basements of secret police. There are screaming nerves in it. Its father is not an animal maleness but some sort of diseased manhood, perverted and rotten. And the writers who offer us this stuff — who must not be confused with those who are dealing fairly and frankly with the more violent aspects of contemporary life — give the game away by their gloating eagerness, the sudden heightening of their descriptive powers. And, let me repeat, in the stories of which I complain, these sadistic antics are displayed for our admiration; it is the Hero, with whom the young reader identifies himself, who is the master of them. Any lad who tries to forget his various frustrations by continually reading such stuff is in danger of real corruption.

(From the *New Statesman and Nation*, July 24, 1954.)

ANGELA CARTER
Once More into the Mangle

They contain practical and explicit advice on sexual problems, and glossy, full-page nudes to cut out and pin up. The nudes are equipped with a variety of phallic props (French loaves or those round-headed Japanese dolls), and they all wear faintly anxious smiles, as if to say: "Am I being erotic enough?" with that prim lack of inhibition peculiar to the Japanese. Full-page ads feature chubby, immensely trustworthy-looking men holding aloft bottles of magic elixir while demanding: "Come too quickly? Having trouble with *your* erection?" One can see at a glance these Japanese comics are not for children.

Indeed, from their contents, they would appear to be directed either at the crazed sex maniac or the dedicated surrealist. The picture strips are a *vade mecum* to the latent content of life — pictorial lexicons of the most ferocious imagery of desire, violence and terror, erupting amid gouts of gore, red-hot from the unconscious. However, it is respectably-suited Mr Average who buys them to flick through on his way home to peaceful tea, evening television and continuous, undisrupted, absolute propriety.

The incidence of death, mutilation and sexual intercourse remains roughly constant in Japanese comic books, whatever the narrative. Each book is an anthology of several stories, plus pin-ups, a doctor's column and humorous cartoons. Though there are no specific war comics in Japan, there are often war stories in these comics (and when they deal with the Pacific war, they are often extremely anti-Japanese): no specific horror comics, but the heritage of the *kwaidan* (the ghostly tale and its hideous goblins) cannot be concealed. On

107

the whole, the adult comics deal either with sex and violence against a background of perspectives of skyscrapers, iconographic representations of present-day Tokyo: or they deal with sex and violence among the pine forests, castles and geisha houses of the glorious but imaginary past. They are printed in black and white, with an occasional use of red, on the usual absorbent paper.

The comics of modern life often contain stories based on incidents which actually happened: the exploits of blackmailing barhostesses, of bank robbers, of gangsters, of embezzlers and of the abductors of schoolgirls. Schoolgirls are a perennial bloom in Japanese erotology, because of their distinctive uniforms, middy blouses, pleated skirts and black stockings, clearly designed by Colette's first husband.

The narratives are stylistically banal and, in the international habit of low art, often take time off to moralise — though the tenor of this moralising can bring the outsider up with a start. Two young girls, in floppy hats, long skirts, high boots, bleached hair and false eyelids, abandon themselves to dissipation. They attend pot parties (where the strip suddenly goes into negative, as in an old-fashioned avant-garde movie): fornicate with pop singers; find only ennui; and conclude their careers by jumping, hand in hand, off a bridge. The last picture, where in mid-air, they endearingly clutch their hats, has this caption: "For life is as fleeting as the dew in the morning and the world is only the dream of a dream."

The technique of all the comics seems to derive rather from the cinema than from American comic-book art, just as the themes relate more to the B feature film than to the self-conscious whimsy of the super-hero comics. Since the strip, as a form, is essentially a series of stills, unfolding only in the personal time of the reader, the effect is one of continuous static convulsion. This is a condition sufficiently approximating to that of modern Japanese society.

Typically, the strip begins with a pre-credit sequence, sometimes spread over two pages. In the period stories, this may show a detailed, picturesque and action-packed panorama of a battle or an execution. In a modern story, it may show the climax of a horse race or a boxing match, or the hero or heroines, or both, in a striking pose (the heroine lying on her back perhaps, with a racing car roaring out between her legs). This is an overture or appetiser.

The narrative itself is composed in a series of long shots, close-ups and angle shots, with an elaborate use of montage. A typical montage sequence in a samurai comic might show: a bird on a bare branch against the moon; the dragon-tailed eaves of a castle roof; an eye; a mouth; a hand holding a sword. Some use is also made of techniques equivalent to panning or tracking shots: for example, a series of different-sized and shaped shots of a night sky with moon and clouds.

It would be possible to use any of the stories as an un-usually detailed shooting script. Latterly, there has been a vogue in Japan for what looks very much like comic-book versions of Italian Westerns, another form that has a heighten-ed emotional intensity and stylised violence.

Some artists, however, use elements of traditional Japanese graphic art. Until the 20th century, there was a flourishing trade in pictorial chapbooks, detailing heroic adventure and tales of life in the brothel quarters. The Japanese script itself is more of a visual medium than the Roman one and tends to sharpen the visual sensibility. The comic books, however transmuted, do not in themselves represent a complete break with tradition or reveal the beginnings of a post-literate period. But it is some indication of the mental relaxation they offer that particularly obscure Chinese characters, when they occur in headlines (though not, for some reason, in the text), often have their phonetic transcription in the syllabic *hiragana* printed in little letters beside them.

The period stories especially often borrow their graphic line from the past. This makes them more beautiful than the modern stories. They also sometimes use calligraphic insertions in especially breathtaking scenes, rather than putting the words in balloons coming from the actors' heads.

What is actually going on in the pictures often looks rather odd to me because I cannot read Japanese. When a translation is provided, it usually turns out to be worse than I could have imagined. Why isn't this girl fighting back during a gang rape? Because they forethoughtfully dislocated all her limbs, first. Why is this weeping old lady in bed with this wild-eyed boy? She is his mother; she has given herself to him as rough-and-ready therapy for his persistent voyeurism. Can this really, truly, be a close-up of a female orifice? Yes. It can.

One also finds the marvellous.

The ceiling of a castle hall is pierced with swords, each grasped in a severed hand that drips blood onto the floor below.

A man the size of a flea plants a kiss on the nipple of a giantess as though it were a flag upon a virgin peak. Waking, she cracks him between her fingers.

A feudal lord, afflicted with ulcers, sees the head of the son he has murdered rising up out of each pustule. In a fatal exorcism attempt, he vigorously scoops the damned spots out with his sword until he falls, gashed in his entirety.

The samurai comics offer the most stunning harvest of sadism, masochism, nervous agitation, disquiet and dread, perhaps because the in-built mythic quality of the pseudo-historic time with which they deal excites creative energy. The hieratic imagery occasionally stuns. The virtue of a low-art form is that it can transcend itself. An artist named Hachiro Tanaka stands out from the visual anonymity of his genre by a style of such blatant eroticism and perverse sophistication that, in the west, he would become a cult and illustrate limited editions of *A Hundred and Thirty Days at Sodom*.

Tanaka perpetrates lyrically bizarre holocausts, in decors simplified to the point of abstraction. His emphasis on decorative elements ‒ the pattern on a screen; on a kimono; that of the complication of combs in a girl's hair ‒ and his marked distortion of human form, create an effect something between Gustave Klimt and Walt Disney. His baby-faced heroines typify Woman as a masochistic object, her usual function in the strips.

Formed only to suffer, she is subjected to every indignity. Forced to take part in group sex where it is hard to tell whose breast belongs to whom, her lush body unwillingly hired out to reptilian and obese old men, the eyes of a Tanaka woman leak tears, and her swollen lips perpetually shape around "o" of woe, until the inevitable denouement, where she is emphatically stuck through with a sword, or her decapitated but still weeping head occupies one of his favourite freeze-frames. But, whichever way the women go, they all go through the mangle — unless they are very wicked indeed; when they obey the Sadean law and live happily ever after.

If the ravaged dove is the norm, Woman in the strips is nevertheless a subtly ambiguous figure. One series specialises in erotic futurology. Again, the artwork is at a high level. The latent content presumably reflects the fears that haunt the doctor's columns. ("How can I enlarge my penis?") A race of superwomen has by-passed the male in its search for sexual gratification, and, in designs of a peculiar purity, uses devices, masterpieces of Japanese technology, such as chairs with breast-massaging hands, and electronic lickers. These last are elongated, quivering tongues on legs that produce spasms of extraordinary delight, though (significantly) they often fuse.

In another context, a fat harpy lolls on a cushion of little crushed men in blue business suits; into her ravenous mouth she crams TV sets, washing machines and all the other booty of the modern industrialised society. Again, an old woman crouches over a sleeping boy, painting a young face on top of her own withered one with juice extracted from her victim. A culture that prefers to keep its women at home is extremely hard on the men.

But human relations either have the stark anonymity of rape or else are essentially tragic. Even at the level of the lowest art, the Japanese, it would seem, cannot bring themselves to borrow that simplistic, European formula: "then they lived happily ever after."

The girl dies from her rape in the arms of the knight who saves her; he walks off alone, Hemingwayesque, into a lonely landscape under a waning moon. The girl and the knight murder the lord who sold her to the brothel; they immolate themselves. The deserted bar-girl consumes sleeping pills. Love is a tragic, fated passion; yet, still, heroically, they love. Japan's is a very romantic culture, even if the Japanese jab enormous daggers in the bellies of the comic strip girls, and flay them alive, and crucify them, and even jump on them six or seven at a time.

The narratives are interspersed with humorous cartoons. A man raises his bowler hat to reveal a bald head topped with a nipple. A determined lover sharpens his penis with a knife, while a girl watches with justifiable apprehension. An extraordinary cartoon, revealing god knows what stresses in the inflexible family structure, shows a baby at the breast sucking its mother literally dry — until she is nothing but a deflated bag of skin. Unabashed scatalogical humour proliferates. A man rises above the door of a cubicle propelled by a rising mountain of his own excrement; unperturbed, he continues to read his newspaper. A man strains and strains and eventually excretes his entire bowel.

Essentially, the comic books are plainly devoted to the uncensored, raw subject-matter of dream. They are obtainable at any bookstall for about 10p. They are not meat for intellectuals; when Yukio Mishima disembowelled himself in public, he can hardly have been influenced by the delirious representations of *seppuku* in the comic books. They are read at idle moments by the people whose daily life is one of perfect gentleness, reticence and kindliness, who speak a language without oaths, and where blasphemy is impossible since the Emperor abdicated his godhead. Few societies lay such stress on public decency and private decorum. Few offer such structured escape valves.

(From *New Society*, April 9, 1971.)

PART THREE
Children's Books and Fear

INTRODUCTION

Most children are frightened by a book or illustration at some time; when they grow to be parents they may want to protect their own off-spring from this experience. Children are, after all, particularly prone to fear; below seven years in the peak period for nightmares, which can be as vivid as reality itself and sometimes mistaken for such.

In this situation, the idea of getting at a child through these fears is now seen as repellent, and Mrs. Sherwood's famous chapter from *The History of the Fairchild Family*, included here, would no longer be tolerated. Even the late Victorians took to omitting it from what otherwise remained a very popular book, although at the time of first publication, it was "realistic rather than terrifying. The gibbet in the lonely wood could still have been seen in 1818 and for the next fourteen years; any child out nutting might have stumbled upon it".*

But however unpleasant now, the chapter quoted seems to me better written and more exciting than anything else in *The History of the Fairchild Family*. The children's quarrel has the immediacy of everyday life, and the prose build-up just before they all come across the gibbet is an effective piece of impressionism. There could be something of a paradox here: some children might be terrified by this chapter; others may like it best of all, finding some of the excitement generated elsewhere in those games where children flirt with their own fears, and in so doing often bring them under better control. There is, undoubtedly, something fascinating about fear; if we demanded stories that never played upon this

* M. Nancy Cutt, *Mrs. Sherwood and her Books for Children*, p. 68 (Oxford University Press, 1974)

115

particular emotion, life – and books – would be much duller. In his essay *The Fear of the Film*, reprinted as the second extract on this subject, G. K. Chesterton is surely right to mock the very idea of listing frightening books from which all children should be protected. As he shows, fear itself can be unpredictable; a child seems bound to feel it one way or another, sometimes from obvious sources, sometimes not.

So, although one can sympathise with the terrors of the young Charles Lamb, so well described in the next extract, *Witches and Night-fears*, there is an ambiguity even here. Elsewhere, he actually refers affectionately to another book of his youth, a "great *Book of Martyrs*", about "good men who chose to be burnt alive" and where a child could play at putting his "hands upon the flames which were pictured in the pretty pictures which the book had, and feel them".* He even has a good word for the rest of Stackhouse's *History of the Bible*, "where there was the picture of the Ark and all the beasts getting into it". Can one ever hope to balance the pleasure this picture gave against the horror brought about by the graphic Witch of Endor in the same volume? Could anyone have guessed that it was going to be this particular illustration, rather than any of the gruesome pictures from the *Book of Martyrs* that would so horrify Lamb as a child? And even if all conceivably frightening books had been hidden away, Lamb himself realises that this would hardly have worked, as his reference to "Dear little T.H." (Thornton Hunt) makes clear. This was the son of Leigh Hunt, who had himself been fearfully teased and frightened by his older brother as a child. Reacting against this as a father, he managed – according to Lamb – to visit almost as bad fears upon his son. As psychoanalysts have often pointed out – and it's interesting to note Lamb's own use of the word 'archetype' here – a child's fantasy life can create demons equal to any picture or prose description. In this sense, reading about horrors may sometimes help put such fears at

---

* E. V. Lucas, *The Life of Charles Lamb*, pp.17-18 (Methuen, 1905)

least into a more helpful context, where a child can begin to refer to them by name, and share his experience with others.

Even so, I doubt whether many people today would be willing to leave pictures around for children, of the horror suggested by Lamb's descriptions. There may be a limit to what any child can cope with at one time; over-graphic pictures of fearsome scenes should perhaps be avoided for the very young. At a time when defences are still being built against excessive fear, it would seem premature to flood them with extra strong stimuli. But then, some adults have always rather enjoyed frightening children, never a very difficult audience to work upon, and the 19th century admonitory novel offered a splendid chance for working off sadistic fantasies on a young audience, all in the name of morality. The young woman whom Dickens describes in *Nurse's Stories,* the next extract, had another motive too: if her young charge could be sufficiently terrified into silence, there would be less chance of any rebellion after lights-out. In the same way, parents through history have made use of Cromwell, Bonaparte, and even the Kaiser in nursery rhymes, as a threat to the child who still won't settle down. The tone of this particular piece by Dickens, however, is difficult to pin down. There is not that wistful melancholy of a Charles Lamb; rather, almost an intoxication of terror, a mixture of fear and thrill. Dickens' blames his nurse for being responsible for "most of the dark corners" in his mind, yet some of her Gothic obsessions are reminiscent of his own fiction. A number of 19th century writers have paid tribute to the subsequent influence on them of some of the rough, frightening stories they heard as a child; could Dickens nurse too have had a stimulating as well as terrifying effect?

The whole topic of books and fear has always seemed to interest people, particularly parents. In *Things that go bump in the Night,* Catherine Storr sums up current thinking on the subject, writing both as a children's author herself, and as a psychiatrist with experience of children.

117

MRS SHERWOOD
Story on the Sixth Commandment

One morning, as Mr. Fairchild was coming downstairs, he heard the little ones quarrelling in the parlour, and he stood still to hearken to what they said.

"You are very cruel, Lucy," said Henry; "why won't you let me play with the doll?"

"What have boys to do with dolls?" said Lucy; "you sha'n't have it."

"But he shall," said Emily; and the door being half open, Mr. Fairchild saw her snatch the doll from her sister, and give it to Henry, who ran with it behind the sofa. Lucy tried to get the doll away from her brother, but Emily ran in between them, and accidentally hurt Lucy's foot, which increased Lucy's anger so much that she pinched her sister's arm; whereupon Emily struck her sister, and I do not know what might have next happened, if Mr. Fairchild had not run in and seized hold of them.

Mr. Fairchild, however, heard Emily say to her sister, "I do not love you, you naughty girl!" and he heard the other reply, "And I don't love you — I am sure I do not!"

At the same time they looked as if what they said was true for the moment; for their faces were red, and their eyes full of anger. Mr. Fairchild took the doll away from Henry, and, taking a rod out of the cupboard, he whipped the hands of all the three children, till they smarted again, saying —

> "Let dogs delight to bark and bite
> For God has made them so;
> Let bears and lions growl and fight,
> For 'tis their nature too.

"But, children, you should never let
Such angry passions rise;
Your little hands were never made
To tear each other's eyes."

After which he made them stand in a corner of the room, without their breakfasts; neither did they get anything to eat all the morning, and, what was worse, their papa and mamma looked very gravely at them. When John came in to lay the cloth for dinner, Mr. Fairchild called the three children to him, and asked them if they were sorry for the wicked things which they had done.

"Oh yes, papa! — yes, papa! we are sorry," they said.

"Do you remember, Lucy — do you remember, Emily," said Mr. Fairchild, "what words you used to each other?"

"Yes, papa," they answered; "we said that we did not love each other; but we did not mean what we said."

"Yes," answered Mr. Fairchild, "you did mean what you said at the time, or else why did you pinch and strike?"

"Oh, papa!" answered Lucy, "because we were angry then."

"And suppose," said Mr. Fairchild, "that you had had a knife in your hand, Lucy, in your anger you might have struck your sister with it, and perhaps have killed her."

"Oh no, papa! — no, papa!" said Lucy; "I would not kill my poor sister for all the world."

Mr. Fairchild. "You would not kill her now, I am sure, for all the world, because you are not now angry with her; nor would you pinch her now, I am sure, but when hatred and anger seize upon persons they do many shocking things which they would not think of at another time. Have you not read how wicked Cain, in his anger, killed his brother Abel? And do you not remember the verse, I John iii. 15: 'Whosoever hateth his brother is a murderer, and ye know that no murderer hath eternal life abiding in him'?"

"Oh, papa, papa!" said Emily, "we will never be angry again."

"My dear Emily," said Mr. Fairchild, "you must not say

that you will never be angry again, but that you will pray to God in the name of the Lord Jesus Christ, your great Redeemer, to send his Holy Spirit into your heart, to take away these wicked passions."

"Papa," said Lucy, "when the Spirit of God is in me, shall I never hate any more, or be in wicked passions any more?"

"My dear child," answered Mr. Fairchild, "the Lord Jesus Christ says, 'By this shall men know that ye are my disciples, if ye have love one towards another,' (John xiii. 35.) Therefore, if ye are followers of the Lord Jesus Christ, and the Spirit of God is in you, you will love everybody, even those who hate and use you ill."

Then Mr. Fairchild kissed his children and forgave them; and they kissed each other; and Mr. Fairchild gave them leave to dine with him as usual. After dinner, Mr. Fairchild said to his wife: —

"I will take the children this evening to Blackwood, and show them something there, which, I think, they will remember as long as they live; and I hope they will take warning from it, and pray more earnestly for new hearts, that they may love each other with perfect and heavenly love."

"If you are going to Blackwood," said Mrs. Fairchild, "I cannot go with you, my dear, though I approve of your taking the children. Let John go with you to carry Henry part of the way; for it is too far for him to walk."

"What is there at Blackwood, papa?" cried the children.

"Something very shocking," said Mrs. Fairchild. "There is one there," said Mr. Fairchild, looking very grave, "who hated his brother."

"Will he hurt us, papa?" said Henry.

"No," said Mr. Fairchild; "he cannot hurt you now."

When the children and John were ready, Mr. Fairchild set out. They went down the lane nearly as far as the village; and then, crossing over a long field, they came in front of a very thick wood.

"This is Blackwood," said Mr. Fairchild, getting over the

stile; "the pathway is almost grown up; nobody likes to come here now."

"What is here, papa?" added the children; "is it very shocking? We are afraid to go on."

"There is nothing here that will hurt you, my dear children," said Mr. Fairchild. "Am I not with you; and do you think I would lead my children into danger?"

"No, papa," said the children; "but mamma said there was something very dreadful in this wood."

Then Lucy and Emily drew behind Mr. Fairchild, and walked close together, and little Henry asked John to carry him. The wood was very thick and dark, and they walked on for half a mile, going down hill all the way. At last they saw, by the light through the trees, that they were come near to the end of the wood; and as they went further on, they saw an old garden wall, some parts of which being broken down they could see, beyond, a large brick house, which, from the fashion of it, seemed as if it might have stood there some hundred years, and now was fallen to ruin. The garden was overgrown with grasses and weeds, the fruit-trees wanted pruning, and it could now hardly be discovered where the walks had been. One of the old chimneys had fallen down, breaking through the roof of the house in one or two places; and the glass windows were broken near the place where the garden wall had fallen. Just between that and the wood stood a gibbet, on which the body of a man hung in chains. The body had not yet fallen to pieces, although it had hung there some years. It had on a blue coat, a silk handkerchief round the neck, with shoes and stockings, and every other part of the dress still entire; but the face of the corpse was so shocking that the children could not look upon it.

"Oh, papa, papa! who is that?" cried the children.

"That is a gibbet," said Mr. Fairchild; "and the man who hangs upon it is a murderer — one who first hated and afterwards killed his brother! When people are found guilty of stealing or murder, they are hanged upon a gallows, and taken down as soon as they are dead; but in some particular cases, when a man has committed a murder, he is hanged in iron chains upon a gibbet till his body falls to pieces, that all who pass by may take warning by the example."

Whilst Mr. Fairchild was speaking, the wind blew strong and shook the body upon the gibbet, rattling the chains by which it hung.

"Oh, let us go, papa!" said the children, pulling Mr. Fairchild's coat.

"Not yet," said Mr. Fairchild; "I must tell you the history of that wretched man before we go from this place."

So saying, he sat down on the stump of an old tree, and the children gathered close round him.

"When I first came into this country, before any of you, my children, were born," said Mr. Fairchild, "there lived, in that old house which you see before you, a widow lady, who had two sons. The place then, though old-fashioned, was neat and flourishing, the garden being full of fine old fruit-trees, and the flower-beds in beautiful order. The old lady kept an excellent table, and was glad to see any of her neighbours who called in upon her. Your mamma and I used often to go and see her, and should have gone oftener, only we could not bear to see the manner in which she brought up her sons. She never sent them to school lest the master should correct them, but hired a person to teach them reading and writing at home. This man, however, was forbidden to punish them. They were allowed to be with the servants in the stable and kitchen, but the servants were ordered not to deny them anything; so they used to call them names, swear at them, and even strike them, and the servants did not dare to answer them lest they should lose their places; the consequence of which was that no good servant would stay to be abused by wicked children.

"From quarrelling with the servants, these angry boys proceeded to quarrel with each other. James, the eldest, despised his brother Roger, because he, as eldest, was to have the house and land: and Roger, in his turn, despised his brother James. As they grew bigger, they became more and

122

more wicked, proud, and stubborn, sullen and undutiful. Their poor mother still loved them so foolishly that she could not see their faults, and would not suffer them to be checked. At length, when they became young men, their hatred of each other rose to such a height that they often would not speak to each other for days together; and sometimes they would quarrel, and almost come to blows, before their mother's face.

"One evening in autumn, after one of these quarrels, James met his brother Roger returning from shooting, just in the place where the gibbet now stands; they were alone, and it was nearly dark. Nobody knows what words passed between them; but the wicked Roger stabbed his brother with a case-knife, and hid the body in a ditch under the garden, well covering it with dry leaves. A year or more passed before it was discovered by whom this dreadful murder was committed. Roger was condemned, and hung upon that gibbet; and the poor old lady, being thus deprived of both her sons, became deranged, and is shut up in a place where such people are confined. Since that time no one has lived in the house, and, indeed, nobody likes to come this way."

"Oh, what a shocking story!" said the children: "and that miserable man who hangs there is Roger, who murdered his brother? Pray let us go, papa."

"We will go immediately," said Mr. Fairchild: "but I wish first to point out to you, my dear children, that these brothers, when they first began to quarrel in their play, as you did this morning, did not think that death, and perhaps hell, would be the end of their quarrels. Our hearts by nature, my dear children," continued Mr. Fairchild, "are full of hatred. People who have not received new hearts do not really love anybody but themselves; and they hate those who have offended them, or those whom they think any way better than themselves. By nature I should hate Sir Charles Noble, because he is a greater man than myself; and you might hate his children, because they are higher than you. By nature, too, I should hate Farmer Greenfield, because he is ten times richer than I am: and even poor John Trueman, because, of all the men in this country, high or low, he is the most esteemed. And take me with my natural heart to heaven, and I should hate every angel and every archangel, above myself; and even the glory of the Almighty God would be hateful to me. But when, through faith in my dying Redeemer, I receive a new heart, by the inspiration of the Holy Spirit of God, my hatred of God and my fellow-creatures will be turned into love: and I shall 'love my enemies, bless them that curse me, do good to them that hate me, and pray for them that despitefully use me and persecute me' (Matt. v. 44); like my beloved Redeemer, who prayed upon the cross for his enemies, saying, 'Father, forgive them; for they know not what they do.' " (Luke xxiii. 34.)

(From *The History of the Fairchild Family,* 1818.)

G. K. CHESTERTON
The Fear of the Film

Long lists are being given of particular cases in which children have suffered in spirits or health from alleged horrors of the kinema. One child is said to have had a fit after seeing a film; another to have been sleepless with some fixed idea taken from a film; another to have killed his father with a carving-knife through having seen a knife used in a film. This may possibly have occurred; though if it did, anybody of common sense would prefer to have details about that particular child, rather than about that particular picture. But what is supposed to be the practical moral of it, in any case? Is it that the young should never see a story with a knife in it? Are they to be brought up in complete ignorance of *The Merchant of Venice* because Shylock flourishes a knife for a highly disagreeable purpose? Are they never to hear of Macbeth, lest it should slowly dawn upon their trembling intelligence that it is a dagger that they see before them? It would be more practical to propose that a child should never see a real carving-knife, and still more practical that he should never see a real father. All that may come; the era of preventive and prophetic science has only begun. We must not be impatient. But when we come to the cases of morbid panic after some particular exhibition, there is yet more reason to clear the mind of cant. It is perfectly true that a child will have the horrors after seeing some particular detail. It is quite equally true that nobody can possibly predict what that detail will be. It certainly need not be anything so obvious as a murder or even a knife. I should have thought anybody who knew anything about children, or for that matter anybody who had been a child, would know that these nightmares are quite incalculable. The hint of horror may come by any chance in any connexion. If the kinema exhibited nothing but views of country vicarages or vegetarian restaurants, the ugly fancy is as likely to be stimulated by these things as by anything else. It is like seeing a face in the carpet; it makes no difference that it is the carpet at the vicarage.

I will give two examples from my own most personal circle; I could give hundreds from hearsay. I know a child who screamed steadily for hours if he had been taken past the Albert Memorial. This was not a precocious precision or excellence in his taste in architecture. Nor was it a premature protest against all that gimcrack German culture which nearly entangled us in the downfall of the barbaric tyranny. It was the fear of something which he himself described with lurid simplicity as The Cow with the India-rubber Tongue. It sounds rather a good title for a creepy short story. At the base of the Albert Memorial (I may explain for those who have never enjoyed that monument) are four groups of statuary representing Europe, Asia, Africa, and America. America especially is very overwhelming; borne onward on a snorting bison who plunges forward in a fury of western progress, and is surrounded with Red Indians, Mexicans, and all sorts of pioneers, O pioneers, armed to the teeth. The child passed this transatlantic tornado with complete coolness and indifference. Europe however is seated on a bull so mild as to look like a cow; the tip of its tongue is showing and happened to be discoloured by weather; suggesting, I suppose, a living thing coming out of the dead marble. Now nobody could possibly foretell that a weather-stain would occur in that particular place, and fill that particular child with that particular fancy. Nobody is likely to propose meeting it by forbidding graven images, like the Moslems and the Jews. Nobody has said (as yet) that it is bad morals to make a picture of a cow. Nobody has even pleaded that it is bad manners for a cow to put its tongue out. These things are utterly beyond calculation; they are also beyond counting, for they occur all over the place, not only to morbid children but to any children. I knew this particular child very well, being a rather older child myself at the time. He certainly was not congenitally timid or feeble-minded; for he risked going to prison to expose the Marconi Scandal and died fighting in the Great War.

Here is another example out of scores. A little girl, now a very normal and cheerful young lady, had an insomnia of insane terror entirely arising from the lyric of "Little Bo-Peep." After an inquisition like that of the confessor or the psychoanalyst, it was found that the word "bleating" had some obscure connexion in her mind with the word "bleeding." There was thus perhaps an added horror in the phrase "heard"; in hearing rather than seeing the flowing of blood. Nobody could possibly provide against that sort of mistake. Nobody could prevent the little girl from hearing about sheep, any more than the little boy from hearing about cows. We might abolish all nursery rhymes; and as they are happy and popular and used with universal success, it is very likely that we shall. But the whole point of the mistake about that phrase is that it might have been a mistake about any phrase. We cannot foresee all the fancies that might arise, not only out of what we say, but of what we do not say. We cannot avoid promising a child a caramel lest he should think we say cannibal, or conceal the very word "hill" lest it should sound like "hell."

All the catalogues and calculations offered us by the party of caution in this controversy are therefore quite worthless. It is perfectly true that examples can be given of a child being frightened of this, that or the other. But we can never be certain of his being frightened of the same thing twice. It is not on the negative side, by making lists of vetoes, that the danger can be avoided; it can never indeed be entirely avoided. We can only fortify the child on the positive side by giving him health and humour and a trust in God; not omitting (what will much mystify the moderns) an intelligent appreciation of the idea of authority, which is only the other side of confidence, and which alone can suddenly and summarily cast out such devils. But we may be sure that most modern people will not look at it in this way. They will think it more scientific to attempt to calculate the incalculable. So soon as they have realized that it is not so simple as it looks, they will try to map it out, however complicated it may be. When they discover that the terrible detail need not be a knife, but might just as well be a fork, they will only say there is a fork complex as well as a knife complex. And that increasing complexity of complexes is the net in which liberty will be taken.

(From *Fancies Versus Fads*, 1923.)

CHARLES LAMB
Witches and other Night-fears

From my childhood I was extremely inquisitive about witches
and witch-stories. My maid, and more legendary aunt, supplied
me with good store. But I shall mention the accident which
directed my curiosity originally into this channel. In my
father's book-closet, the *History of the Bible*, by Stackhouse,
occupied a distinguished station. The pictures with which it
abounds — one of the ark, in particular, and another of
Solomon's temple, delineated with all the fidelity of ocular
admeasurement, as if the artist had been upon the spot —
attracted my childish attention. There was a picture, too, of
the Witch raising up Samuel, which I wish that I had never
seen. . . .

I was dreadfully alive to nervous terrors. The night-time
solitude, and the dark, were my hell. The suffering I en-
dured in this nature would justify the expression. I never
laid my head on my pillow, I suppose, from the fourth to the
seventh or eighth year of my life — so far as memory serves
in things so long ago — without an assurance, which realized
its own prophecy, of seeing some frightful spectre. Be old
Stackhouse then acquitted in part, if I say, that to his picture
of the Witch raising up Samuel — (O that old man covered
with a mantle!) I owe — not my midnight terrors, the hell of
my infancy — but the shape and manner of their visitation. It
was he who dressed up for me a hag that nightly sate upon
my pillow — a sure bed-fellow, when my aunt or my maid was
far from me. All day long, while the book was permitted me,
I dreamed waking over his delineation, and at night (if I may
use so bold an expression) awoke into sleep, and found the
vision true. I durst not, even in the day-light, once enter the

chamber where I slept, without my face turned to the window, aversely from the bed where my witch-ridden pillow was. — Parents do not know what they do when they leave tender babes alone to go to sleep in the dark. The feeling about for a friendly arm — the hoping for a familiar voice — when they wake screaming — and find none to soothe them — what a terrible shaking it is to their poor nerces! The keeping them up till midnight, through candle-light and the unwholesome hours, as they are called, — would, I am satisifed, in a medical point of view, prove the better caution. — That detestable picture, as I have said, gave the fashion to my dreams — if derams they were — for the scene of them was invariably the room in which I lay. Had I never met with the picture, the fears would have come self-pictured in some shape or other —

Headless bear, black man, or ape —

but, as it was, my imaginations took that form. — It is not book, or picture, or the stories of foolish servants, which create these terrors in children. They can at most but give them a direction. Dear little T. H. who of all children has been brought up with the most scrupulous exlcusion of every taint of superstition — who was never allowed to hear of goblin or apparition, or scarcely to be told of bad men, or to read or hear of any distressing story — finds all this world of fear, from which he has been so rigidly excluded *ab extra*, in his own "thick-coming fancies;" and from his little midnight pillow, this nurse-child of optimism will start at shapes, unborrowed of tradition, in sweats to which the reveries of the cell-damned murderer are tranquillity.

Gorgons, and Hydras, and Chimæras — dire stories of Celæno and the Harpies — may reproduce themselves in the brain of supersition — but they were there before. They are transcripts, types — the archetypes are in us, and eternal. How else should the recital of that, which we know in a waking sense to be false, come to affect us at all? — or

—Names, whose sense we see not,
Fray us with things that be not?

Is it that we naturally conceive terror from such objects, considered in their capacity of being able to inflict upon us bodily injury? — O, least of all! These terrors are of older standing. They date beyond body — or, without the body, they would have been the same. All the cruel, tormenting, defined devils in Dante — tearing, mangling, choking, stifling, scorching demons — are they one half so fearful to the spirit of a man, as the simple idea of a spirit unembodied following him —

> Like one that on a lonesome road
> Doth walk in fear and dread,
> And having once turn'd round, walks on,
> And turns no more his head;
> Because he knows a frightful fiend
> Doth close behind him tread.

(From *The Essays of Elia*, 1823.)

131

CHARLES DICKENS
Nurse's Stories

. . . But, when I was at Dullborough one day, revisiting the
associations of my childhood as recorded in previous pages
of these notes, my experience in this wise was made quite
inconsiderable and of no account, by the quantity of places
and people — utterly impossible places and people, but none
the less alarmingly real — that I found I had been introduced
to by my nurse before I was six years old, and used to be
forced to go back to at night without at all wanting to go.
If we all knew our own minds (in a more enlarged sense than
the popular acceptation of that phrase), I suspect we should
find our nurses responsible for most of the dark corners we
are forced to go back to, against our wills.

The first diabolical character who intruded himself on my
peaceful youth (as I called to mind that day at Dullborough),
was a certain Captain Murderer. This wretch must have been
an offshoot of the Blue Beard family, but I had no suspicion
of the consanguinity in those times. His warning name would
seem to have awakened no general prejudice against him, for
he was admitted into the best society and possessed immense
wealth. Captain Murderer's mission was matrimony, and the
gratification of a cannibal appetite with tender brides. On his
marriage morning, he always caused both sides of the way to
church to be planted with curious flowers; and when his
bride said, "Dear Captain Murderer, I never saw flowers like
these before: what are they called?" he answered, "They are
called Garnish for house-lamb," and laughed at his ferocious
practical joke in a horrid manner, disquieting the minds of the
noble bridal company, with a very sharp show of teeth, then
displayed for the first time. He made love in a coach and six,

and married in a coach and twelve, and all his horses were milk-white horses with one red spot on the back which he caused to be hidden by the harness. For, the spot *would* come there, though every horse was milk-white when Captain Murderer bought him. And the spot was young bride's blood. (To this terrific point I am indebted for my first personal experience of a shudder and cold beads on the forehead.) When Captain Murderer had made an end of feasting and revelry, and had dismissed the noble guests, and was alone with his wife on the day month after their marriage, it was his whimsical custom to produce a golden rolling-pin and a silver pie-board. Now, there was this special feature in the Captain's courtships, that he always asked if the young lady could make pie-crust; and if she couldn't by nature or education, she was taught. Well. When the bride saw Captain Murderer produce the golden rolling-pin and silver pie-board, she remembered this, and turned up her laced milk sleeves to make a pie. The Captain brought out a silver pie-dish of immense capacity, and the Captain brought out flour and butter and eggs and all things needful, except the inside of the pie; of materials for the staple of the pie itself, the Captain brought out none. Then said the lovely bride, "Dear Captain Murderer, what pie is this to be?" He replied, "A meat pie." Then said the lovely bride, "Dear Captain Murderer, I see no meat." The Captain humorously retorted, "Look in the glass." She looked in the glass, but still she saw no meat, and then the Captain roared with laughter, and suddenly frowning and drawing his sword, bade her roll out the crust. So she rolled out the crust, dropping large tears upon it all the time because he was so cross, and when she had lined the dish with crust and had cut the crust all ready to fit the top, the Captain called out, "*I* see the meat in the glass!" And the bride looked up at the glass, just in time to see the Captain cutting her head off; and he chopped her in pieces, and peppered her, and salted her, and put her in the pie, and sent it to the baker's, and ate it all, and picked the bones.

Captain Murderer went on in this way, prospering

exceedingly, until he came to choose a birde from two twin sisters, and at first didn't know which to choose. For, though one was fair and the other dark, they were both equally beautiful. But the fair twin loved him, and the dark twin hated him, so he chose the fair one. The dark twin would have prevented the marriage if she could, but she couldn't; however, on the night before it, much suspecting Captain Murderer, she stole out and climbed his garden wall, and looked in at his window through a chink in the shutter, and saw him having his teeth filed sharp. Next day she listened all day, and heard him make his joke about the house-lamb. And that day month, he had the paste rolled out, and cut the fair twin's head off, and chopped her in pieces, and peppered her, and salted her, and put her in the pie, and sent it to the baker's, and ate it all, and picked the bones.

Now, the dark twin had had her suspicions much increased by the filing of the Captain's teeth, and again by the house-lamb joke. Putting all things together when he gave out that her sister was dead, she divined the truth, and determined to be revenged. So, she went up to Captain Murderer's house, and knocked at the knocker and pulled at the bell, and when the Captain came to the door, said: "Dear Captain Murderer, marry me next, for I always loved you and was jealous of my sister." The Captain took it as a compliment, and made a polite answer, and the marriage was quickly arranged. On the night before it, the bride again climbed to his window, and again saw him having his teeth filed sharp. At this sight she laughed such a terrible laugh at the chink in the shutter, that the Captain's blood curdled, and he said: "I hope nothing has disagreed with me!" At that, she laughed again, a still more terrible laugh, and the shutter was opened and search made, but she was nimbly gone, and there was no one. Next day they went to church in a coach and twelve, and were married. And that day month, she rolled the pie-crust out, and Captain Murderer cut her head off, and chopped her in pieces, and peppered her, and salted her, and put her in the pie, and sent it to the baker's, and ate it all, and picked the bones.

But before she began to roll out the paste she had taken a deadly poison of a most awful character, distilled from toads' eyes and spiders' knees; and Captain Murderer had hardly picked her last bone, when he began to swell, and to turn blue, and to be all over spots, and to scream. And he went on swelling and turning bluer, and being more all over spots and screaming, until he reached from floor to ceiling and from wall to wall; and then, at one o'clock in the morning, he blew up with a loud explosion. At the sound of it, all the milk-white horses in the stables broke their halters and went mad, and then they galloped over everybody in Captain Murderer's house (beginning with the family blacksmith who had filed his teeth) until the whole were dead, and then they galloped away.

Hundreds of times did I hear this legend of Captain Murderer, in my early youth, and added hundreds of times was there a mental compulsion upon me in bed, to peep in at his window as the dark twin peeped, and to revisit his horrible house, and look at him in his blue and spotty and screaming stage, as he reached from floor to ceiling and from wall to wall. The young woman who brought me acquainted with Captain Murderer had a fiendish enjoyment of my terrors, and used to begin, I remember — as a sort of introductory overture — by clawing the air with both hands, and uttering a long low hollow groan. So acutely did I suffer from this ceremony in combination with this infernal Captain, that I sometimes used to plead I thought I was hardly strong enough and old enough to hear the story again just yet. But, she never spared me one word of it, and indeed commended the awful chalice to my lips as the only preservative known to science against "The Black Cat" — a weird and glaring-eyed supernatural Tom, who was reputed to prowl about the world by night, sucking the breath of infancy, and who was endowed with a special thirst (as I was given to understand) for mine.

This female bard — may she have been repaid my debt of obligation to her in the matter of nightmares and perspirations!

— reappears in my memory as the daughter of a shipwright. Her name was Mercy, though she had none on me. There was something of a shipbuilding flavour in the following story. As it always recurs to me in a vague association with calomel pills, I believe it to have been reserved for dull nights when I was low with medicine.

There was once a shipwright, and he wrought in a Government Yard, and his name was Chips. And his father's name before him was Chips, and *his* father's name before *him* was Chips, and they were all Chipses. And Chips the father had sold himself to the Devil for an iron pot and a bushel of tenpenny nails and half a ton of copper and a rat that could speak; and Chips the grandfather had sold himself to the Devil for an iron pot and a bushel of tenpenny nails and half a ton of copper and a rat that could speak; and Chips the great-grandfather had disposed of himself in the same direction on the same terms; and the bargain had run in the family for a long long time. So, one day, when young Chips was at work in the Dock Slip all alone, down in the dark hold of an old Seventy-four that was haled up for repairs, the Devil presented himself, and remarked:

> "A Lemon has pips,
> And a Yard has ships,
> And *I*'ll have Chips!"

(I don't know why, but this fact of the Devil's expressing himself in rhyme was peculiarly trying to me.) Chips looked up when he heard the words, and there he saw the Devil with saucer eyes that squinted on a terrible great scale, and that struck out sparks of blue fire continually. 'And whenever he winked his eyes, showers of blue sparks came out, and his eyelashes made a clattering like flints and steels striking lights. And hanging over one of his arms by the handle was an iron pot, and under that arm was a bushel of tenpenny nails, and under his other arm was half a ton of copper, and sitting on one of his shoulders was a rat that could speak. So, the Devil said again:

"A Lemon has pips,
And a Yard has ships,
And *I*'ll have Chips!"

(The invariable effect of this alarming tautology on the part
of the Evil Spirit was to deprive me of my senses for some
moments.) So, Chips answered never a word, but went on
with his work. "What are you doing, Chips?" said the rat that
could speak. "I am putting in new planks where you and your
gang have eaten old away," said Chips. "But we'll eat them
too," said the rat that could speak; "and we'll let in the water
and drown the crew, and we'll eat them too." Chips, being
only a shipwright, and not a Man-of-war's man, said, "You
are welcome to it." But he couldn't keep his eyes off the half
a ton of copper or the bushel of tenpenny nails; for nails and
copper are a shipwright's sweethearts, and shipwrights will run
away with them whenever they can. So, the Devil said, "I see
what you are looking at, Chips. You had better strike the
bargain. You know the terms. Your father before you was
well acquainted with them, and so were your grandfather and
great-grandfather before him." Says Chips, "I like the copper,
and I like the nails, and I don't mind the pot, but I don't
like the rat." Says the Devil, fiercely, "You can't have the
metal without him — and *he's* a curiosity. I'm going." Chips,
afraid of losing the half a ton of copper and the bushel of
nails, then said, "Give us hold!" So, he got the copper and
the nails and the pot and the rat that could speak, and the
Devil vanished. Chips sold the copper, and he sold the nails,
and he would have sold the pot; but whenever he offered it
for sale, the rat was in it, and the dealers dropped it, and
would have nothing to say to the bargain. So, Chips resolved
to kill the rat, and, being at work in the Yard one day with a
great kettle of hot pitch on one side of him and the iron pot
with the rat in it on the other, he turned the scalding pitch
into the pot, and filled it full. Then, he kept his eye upon it
till it cooled and hardened, and then he let it stand for twenty
days, and then he heated the pitch again and turned it back

into the kettle, and then he sank the pot in water for twenty days more, and then he got the smelters to put it in the furnace for twenty days more, and then they gave it him out, red hot, and looking like red-hot glass instead of iron — yet there was the rat in it, just the same as ever! And the moment it caught his eye, it said with a jeer:

> "A Lemon has pips,
> And a Yard has ships,
> And *I*'ll have Chips!"

(For this Refrain I had waited since its last appearance, with inexpressible horror, which now culminated.) Chips now felt certain in his own mind that the rat would stick to him; the rat, answering his thought, said, "I will — like pitch!"

Now, as the rat leaped out of the pot when it had spoken, and made off, Chips began to hope that it wouldn't keep its word. But, a terrible thing happened next day. For, when dinner-time came, and the Dock-bell rang to strike work, he put his rule into the long pocket at the side of his trousers, and there he found a rat — not that rat, but another rat. And in his hat, he found another; and in his pocket-handkerchief, another; and in the sleeves of his coat, when he pulled it on to go to dinner, two more. And from that time he found himself so frightfully intimate with all the rats in the Yard, that they climbed up his legs when he was at work, and sat on his tools while he used them. And they could all speak to one another, and he understood what they said. And they got into his lodging, and into his bed, and into his teapot, and into his beer, and into his boots. And he was going to be married to a corn-chandler's daughter; and when he gave her a workbox he had himself made for her, a rat jumped out of it; and when he put his arm round her waist, a rat clung about her; so the marriage was broken off, though the banns were already twice put up — which the parish clerk well remembers, for, as he handed the book to the clergyman for the second time of asking, a large fat rat ran over the leaf. (By this time a special cascade of rats was rolling down my back, and the whole of my small listening person was overrun with them. At intervals ever since, I have been morbidly afraid of my own pocket, lest my exploring hand should find a specimen or two of those vermin in it.)

You may believe that all this was very terrible to Chips; but even all this was not the worst. He knew besides, what the rats were doing, wherever they were. So, sometimes he would cry aloud, when he was at his club at night, "Oh! Keep the rats out of the convicts' burying-ground! Don't let them do that!" Or, "There's one of them at the cheese downstairs!" Or, "There's two of them smelling at the baby in the garret!" Or, other things of that sort. At last, he was voted mad, and lost his work in the Yard, and could get no other work. But King George wanted men, so before very long he got pressed for a sailor. And so he was taken off in a boat one evening to his ship, lying at Spithead, ready to sail. And so the first thing he made out in her as he got near her, was the figure-head of the old Seventy-four, where he had seen the Devil. She was called the Argonaut, and they rowed right under the bowsprit where the figure-head of the Argonaut, with a sheepskin in his hand and a blue gown on, was looking out to sea; and sitting staring on his forehead was the rat who could speak, and his exact words were these: "Chips ahoy! Old boy! We've pretty well eat them too, and we'll drown the crew, and will eat them too!" (Here I always became exceedingly faint, and would have asked for water, but that I was speechless.)

The ship was bound for the Indies; and if you don't know where that is, you ought to it, and angels will never love you. (Here I felt myself an outcast from a future state.) The ship set sail that very night, and she sailed, and sailed, and sailed. Chips's feelings were dreadful. Nothing ever equalled his terrors. No wonder. At last, one day he asked leave to speak to the Admiral. The Admiral giv' leave. Chips went down on his knees in the Great State Cabin. "Your Honour, unless your Honour, without a moment's loss of time, makes sail for the nearest shore, this is a doomed ship, and her name is the Coffin!" "Young man, your words are a madman's words." "Your Honour, no; they are nibbling us away." "They?" "Your Honour, them dreadful rats. Dust and hollowness where solid oak ought to be! Rats nibbling a grave for every man on board! Oh! Does your Honour love your Lady and your pretty children?" "Yes, my man, to be sure." "Then, for God's sake, make for the nearest shore, for at this present moment the rats are all stopping in their work, and are all looking straight towards you with bare teeth, and are all saying to one another that you shall never, never, never, never, see your Lady and your children more." "My poor fellow, you are a case for the doctor. Sentry, take care of this man!"

So, he was bled and he was blistered, and he was this and that, for six whole days and nights. So, then he again asked leave to speak to the Admiral. The Admiral giv' leave. He went down on his knees in the Great State Cabin. "Now, Admiral, you must die! You took no warning; you must die! The rats are never wrong in their calculations, and they make out that they'll be through, at twelve to-night. So, you must die! — With me and all the rest!" And so at twelve o'clock there was a great leak reported in the ship, and a torrent of water rushed in and nothing could stop it, and they all went down, every living soul. And what the rats — being water-rats — left of Chips, at last floated to shore, and sitting on him was an immense overgrown rat, laughing, that dived when the corpse touched the beach and never came up. And there was a deal of seaweed on the remains. And if you get thirteen bits of seaweed, and dry them and burn them in the fire, they will go off like in these thirteen words as plain as plain can be:

> "A Lemon has pips,
> And a Yard has ships,
> And I've got Chips!"

The same female bard — descended, possibly, from those terrible old Scalds who seem to have existed for the express purpose of addling the brains of mankind when they begin to investigate languages — made a standing pretence which greatly assisted in forcing me back to a number of hideous places that I would by all means have avoided. This pretence was, that all her ghost stories had occurred to her own relations. Politeness towards a meritorious family, therefore, forbade my doubting them, and they acquired an air of authentication that impaired my digestive powers for life. There was a narrative concerning an unearthly animal foreboding death, which appeared in the open street to a parlour-maid who "went to fetch the beer" for supper; first (as I now recall it) assuming the likeness of a black dog, and gradually rising on its hind-legs and swelling into the semblance of some quadruped greatly surpassing a hippopotamus: which apparition — not because I deemed it in the least improbable, but because I felt it to be really too large to bear — I feebly endeavoured to explain away. But, on Mercy's retorting with wounded dignity that the parlour-maid was her own sister-in-law, I perceived there was no hope, and resigned myself to this zoological phenomenon as one of my many pursuers. There was another narrative describing the apparition of a young woman who came out of a glass-case and haunted another young woman until the other young woman questioned it and elicited that its bones (Lord! To think of its being so particular about its bones!) were buried under the glass-case, whereas she required them to be interred, with every Undertaking solemnity up to twenty-four pound ten, in another particular place. This narrative I considered I had a personal interest in disproving, because we had glass-cases at home, and how, otherwise, was I to be guaranteed from the intrusion of young women requiring *me* to bury them up to twenty-four pound ten, when I had only twopence a week? But my remorseless nurse cut the ground from under my tender feet, by informing me that She was the other young woman; and I couldn't say "I don't believe you;" it was not possible.

Such are a few of the uncommercial journeys that I was

forced to make, against my will, when I was very young and unreasoning. And really, as to the latter part of them, it is not so very long ago — now I come to think of it — that I was asked to undertake them once again, with a steady countenance.

(From *The Uncommercial Traveller*, 1867.)

CATHERINE STORR
Things that go bump in the Night

It seems curious that in a society like ours, obsessed by the omniscience of scientists and pathetically reliant on the information provided by statistical surveys, we have reached no conclusions about what scenes or ideas in books or on film might damage our children. Every now and then the subject is revived with new force, when some fresh piece of evidence turns up that suggests that violence or sex in one of these mediums has triggered off a peculiarly horrifying act of the same sort. But we don't really know the answers. The most comprehensive piece of research yet to be published was headed by Hilde Himmelweit and concerned the effects on children of watching television. But the report was published in 1958, and television programmes, films and books have changed a good deal since then.

In considering the effect of television on the child, the Himmelweit Commission found that a more important factor than the degree of violence, cruelty or horror shown was the context in which it appeared. Where the background of events was fairly remote from the child's experience, either in space or time, he was not disturbed even by quite horrific actions or circumstances; but this wasn't so if the setting were more like his own life (disturbance here was measured by subsequent anxiety and fear). He could tolerate cowboys and Indians, or Cavaliers and Roundheads killing each other, better than a minor accident in a programme about children in a modern European town.

It is a question of identification. Though the child may identify with the Goodies in any programme, he apparently doesn't on this account feel threatened by the Baddies unless

143

they are operating in a world closely related to the one with which he is familiar. As for violence on the screen provoking violent behaviour in real life, the Himmelweit Commission came to the conclusion that "these programmes will not make normal children delinquent, though they may have an effect on latent delinquents" – a finding confirmed by a piece of research prepared for the Home Office last year. So there is not much help from the psychologists and, as every parent and teacher knows, there are no rules among children themselves. Why is it that a child who can read the most bloodthirsty of the Grimm fairy stories without flinching, is reduced to a pulp of tears by *Black Beauty* and terrified by an illustration of a water nymph? Why can one child read ghost stories with impunity, while another can't even have the volume in the same room, yet both agree in finding Blind Pew from *Treasure Island* the most terrifying character in fiction? Why is the under-the-bed monster for this child a wolf, for that a snake, and for the third a "spider the size of a small kitten"? The answer is that we don't know. We don't know what will frighten, what will depress (more serious in my view) or what will pervert. Apart from the broadest general guide lines, we can only guess; even for one particular child whom we know well, we can never be sure.

I suppose our anxiety about this problem is at least partly due to the psycho-analytical approach to everything, literature and children included, which has grown in this century. Certainly our predecessors were not nearly as fearful of upsetting young readers. We may think of ours as a permissive society, but what the Victorians fed to their children – thinly disguised as entertainment in many cases – smacks of a much greater permissiveness than we enjoy. Death was then, of course, a common occurrence in a child's life, but I'm not sure that this wholly accounts for the regularity with which it turns up in their books, nor for the loving detail which surrounds the deathbed scene. And it wasn't only death; extreme poverty, brutality, idiocy, alcoholism and injustice also play their part.

The settings were contemporary and the victims children. The effect is deliberately sought.

Mrs Randolph, in *Melbourne House* by Elizabeth Wetherill, whips her little daughter till the blood comes, to punish her for not saying grace before meat. The 12-year-old heroine of *A Basket of Flowers* remains imprisoned under sentence of death for some time before her innocence is proved — it wasn't she who stole the brooch, it was a magpie. Four-year-old Sophie, in *Les Malheurs de Sophie*, who disobeyed her mama's instructions not to lag behind on a country walk, is simply left behind to be attacked by the wolves in consequence; no-one sees to it that she doesn't suffer the direct results of being naughty. It seems as if the rules in force in those days about terror and the young may have been not unlike ours today on obscenity. The 19th-century child might be scared out of his wits, as long as he was also uplifted morally, and nowadays we may be corrupted if we are thereby titillated into culture.

It is interesting that the Victorians didn't carry their realistic attitude to children into every possible field. The one subject which was absolutely barred was sex. Birth features prominently, but there are no preliminaries; babies arrive unannounced and the parents seem as much taken by surprise as anyone. But this was a piece of backsliding which belonged to the mid-19th century. The earlier writers had a much more robust approach. Marryat's Midshipman Easy was suckled by what would now be called an unmarried mother, and there's a charming scene in one of his books when a European host, stationed in the tropics, offers a lady of the district some breast of chicken and is reproved for his indelicacy; he should have said "bosom of chicken". Ballantyne, writing a little later, beautifully exemplifies my point. When describing the customs of the savages who inhabit Coral Island and the neighbouring shores, he merely mentions the local practice of polygamy, and then goes on to discuss the morality of the custom of all the chief's wives killing themselves on his death. But he gives a detailed and horrible description of the occasion when a victorious army launch their canoes over the living bodies of their vanquished opponents. Sex was taboo, but torture was O.K.

It is easy to ridicule the fashions of other days, less easy to accept those of our own. It is also difficult to assess *now* exactly what impact a fashionable attitude might have had *then*. Perhaps to the literate Victorian child, secure in his upper- or middle-class home, the horrors of cruelty and poverty seemed far removed from his probable experience. But it is different for children today. The class barriers are not so absolute, literacy is more widely spread and, at the same time, because of radio and television, less essential to the purposes of entertainment and learning. Before they can read, our children have the opportunity to learn about the topics which engross the adult world, and to absorb the prevalent attitudes towards those topics. Are they disturbed by them. If not, we must ask whether perhaps they ought to be? So our problem of censorship becomes extended: we have to consider not only what will frighten children and make them anxious, but also whether we are going to allow this to happen. And, if we are, in what terms we shall speak to them of terror and fear.

I believe that children should be allowed to feel fear. And I believe that they must also be allowed to meet terror and pity and evil. I was delighted to learn last summer from Kaye Webb that her friend Walter de la Mare had told her he believed that children were impoverished if they were protected from everything that might frighten them. He said that the child who hadn't known fear could never be a poet. I would add to that the worldwide folk story of *The Boy Who Didn't Know Fear*. This boy is a sort of guileless simpleton, of the kind often met with in folklore, who is brave because he doesn't foresee dangers. He can spend a night in the belfry with hobgoblins without a tremor because until he is actually attacked (when he defends himself) he recognises no threat. In fact, he is without imagination, that fatal human quality which makes cowards of us all. In one more sophisticated version of this tale the boy wins himself a royal bride through his senseless bravery, but the marriage doesn't prosper because he can still feel no fear. It is the princess's maid who cures the young husband's inadequacy, by pouring cold water over him as he wakes up so that at last, as the story puts it, he learns to shiver.

Wagner used this idea of the hero without fear — and without knowledge — in Siegfried, who discovers man's true nature when he meets his first woman, disrobing Brunnhilde of her shield on the top of her fiery rock with the immortal words "*Das ist kein Mann!*" The myth seems to me true, though not in its obvious meaning for most animals know the meaning of physical fear; but it expresses in the language of poetry the human need for an understanding of more than meets the eye, for the power to speculate and to fantasise. The child must be allowed to day-dream; and if he can dream of what he wants and of the pleasurable things that may come, he will inevitably have his nightmares too.

Once one has answered this basic question, of whether or not children are to be made aware of evil, the second problem arises of how it is to be presented. This is really a technical problem which has to be faced by every writer for children over the age of infancy. Very small children do not require, in fact find it difficult to follow, a plot. It is enough for them to hear the relation of everyday events such as happen to themselves. I've always suspected that the adult liking for factual books about a period within one's own memory springs from the feeling that one has assisted at something that has been considered worthy to be called history. Perhaps the infant who follows the tale of the child who visits his aunt in the country and finds for himself a large brown egg experiences the same pleasure. But by the time they have reached the *Little Black Sambo* age, there has to be a story; where there is a story, there must be conflict and where there is conflict, there must be Good and Evil, in however watered down a version. The Good presents no difficulties; it is, of course, oneself. But how does one feature the Evil?

You can do it in the Ian Fleming style. You can have a tale of smugglers, or dope-pedlars, or spies or a more ordinary brand of crooks, who are totally evil, totally wrong, totally unbelievable. But in a fast-moving, rattling yarn they will pass muster. In this category I would put the Buchan stories, Fleming, of course, and a good many other cops and robbers, Goodies and Baddies types. Everything is seen in the greatest possible contrast, so stark a black and white that nothing is the colour of reality. If it is done well enough you cannot put it down. But it leaves no permanent mark. This is both its weakness and its measure of security. However horrific the horror, it is unbelievable, two-dimensional. It never gets under the skin. In general this sort of book doesn't terrify; its innocuousness is in inverse proportion to its realism.

Or you can de-humanise the enemy and pit your hero against Fate in the shape of either the forces of nature, or the evils of society. Here there need be no loss of reality; man is indeed often faced by natural disasters such as fire, flood, disease and death, and social dangers like war, poverty, ignorance, prejudice and stupidity. I suppose the most outstanding example of this kind of writing is *Robinson Crusoe*. One of the marvellous things about Defoe's manner of telling the story is the contrast he draws between the almost unique situation of the hero and his essential ordinariness.

Several writers for children today use this method of casting Fate as the villain: Hester Burton has written of a great flood, Veronique Day of a landslide, Rutgers van der Loeff of an avalanche. And I think one could include here stories of animals where the animals aren't humanised: not *The Wind in the Willows* or *The Jungle Books*, but *My Friend Flicka* and *The Yearling*, because here the enemies are the natural ones of predators, illness and death.

The evils of society are kept impersonal with more difficulty; it can be tempting to identify the horrors of war with the bestiality of the people you are fighting, or to attribute the misery of poverty to the heartlessness of the rich. But neither Ian Serrailier, in *The Silver Sword*, nor Paul Berna in *They Didn't Come Back*, has vilified people; in both these books about the aftermath of the last war, it is made clear that it is the international situation that separates families, raises suspicion between friends and neighbours, and sends the innocent to be slaughtered. In a totally different context John Rowe Townsend — particularly in *Gumble's Yard*, and in his last book, *The Intruder* — shows that poverty and stupidity are as threatening and as dangerous as personal malice. No child is going to have nightmares about the characters in these books, but any child might learn from them something of the nature of the impersonal evils he may encounter.

Unreality and impersonality; a third approach is humour. If you laugh at your villain you can still use his actions as a necessary impetus to the plot, but to a certain extent you reduce his horror. Erich Kastner does this beautifully in *Emil and The Detectives*, James Barrie was less successful with the Old Etonian, Captain Hook. Another writer who ridicules villainy, though the tone of most of his books is not comic but deeply serious and moving, is Leon Garfield. He involves his readers in a situation where, identified with the hero, they see the forces of evil moving to engulf them and then, suddenly, by a delicate twist of phrase, he shows not the wickedness of the villain but his weakness and, above all, his vanity. As Thackeray pointed out, once you understand a man's vanity, he is in your power; for this reason the Garfield villains evoke almost as much sympathy as terror.

They are also distanced by time, and this is the fourth way in which evil can be depicted without the danger of overwhelming the child participant. If you are writing of a period of history very remote from the present, there is enough space between what happened then and what could happen now to prevent your readers from feeling too much threat to themselves both immediately and personally. So a first-class writer like Rosemary Sutcliff, author of many well-known historical novels, can treat desperate situations with complete realism. She never minimises danger, but in her stories the passage of time serves the same function as the proscenium arch or the spotlight in the theatre; it enables the audience to believe in what is happening on stage while retaining the consciousness of immunity from danger.

Finally there is fantasy; the means of expression which I find most sympathetic, and the easiest to use. Not for adults; fantasy for adults can so quickly degenerate into whimsy or become portentously heavy, perhaps because adults like a clear indication of whether this is meant to be truth or not; they don't tolerate uncertainty well, they like their portions definitely labelled. But children don't make this distinction between fact and imagination. They can move without trouble from one to the other, recognising the value of both.

It is a dichotomy that most of us never lose altogether, though we often deny it. It is seen frequently in patients with terminal illnesses, who demand to be told whether they are dying. To some of these questioners it is right to speak openly, giving one's own guess of their short expectation of life, but there are others who feel obliged to ask to whom it would be cruel and unnecessary to return a truthful answer. I have known people, one with medical degrees, who continued to believe, as Jung said one should, in the face of symptoms which they couldn't help but recognise, that they had a thousand years more to live. Hjalmar Ekdal, in Ibsen's *Wild Duck*, is one of those blind do-gooders who insists on telling everyone the truth, he won't admit the necessity most of us have to believe in what makes life possible, what will keep us sane, in defiance of the evidence. Of course, it might be better, or more admirable, if we were to face the cold facts of our lives with courage and without hope.

If this is a digression it is an important one, because it is this ability to accept two different sorts of truth at the same time, so much more evident in children than in adults, which provides the answer — for me — to the problem of how to tell children of horror and fear. Much of the telling should be in the language of poetry, the language of symbols, because in in this language we can talk to the child of what he needs to know both more economically and at greater depth than in any other. And what he needs to learn includes not only what threatens him from outside, but also his own responses. While we hold his attention with the story, we are communicating at the same time with all sorts of half-conscious feelings that force him to recognise his own involvement.

Perhaps fantasy is the wrong word for this sort of writing; for no single supernatural event need be incorporated in it, but it has magic, the magic of imagination. In *A Dog So Small* nothing happens that can't be explained in factual terms, but besides telling the story of a boy who passionately wants to own a dog, Philippa Pearce is writing of the gap between promise and its fulfilment, of the necessity of fantasy, and of the adjustment to cold sober reality which every dreamer must make. But if she had written down these lessons in flat statements, who would read them? They would be as easily shrugged off as Dracula or Goldfinger, they would be seen to have validity, but no personal relevance.

If we are going to tell children about evil we owe it to them to give the subject its proper importance, just as we should if we were writing about beauty or goodness or truth. We shall succeed in doing this only if we address the child's inner ear, if we can evoke in him, as he reads, that shock of recognition which means the discovery of a fresh aspect of oneself. Because this is one of the things we must say about evil; that it is not always over there, a characteristic of other people but not of ourselves. Evil is within as well as without, and by understanding our own feelings we have the power over evil in others that understanding gives.

There is one last point. If we talk to children about the great subjects in this way, in folk stories and myths and in any form of art which exercises the imagination, we are giving them something else besides the fruit of consciousness, the knowledge of good and evil. We are demonstrating also a way of handling this knowledge which makes it tolerable to live with. We are showing that it can be used as one of the elements of creative art to make a pattern in which both the good and the bad are essential. This is the true magic.

(From the *Sunday Times Magazine*, March 7, 1971.)

PART FOUR
Children's Classics and some Controversies

INTRODUCTION

The concept of a favourite or classic children's book has often been something of a false friend to many young readers over the years. Adults are good at stocking libraries or buying as gifts books they remember as once having liked, but which, later, have little to say to contemporary children (and, who knows, may also have bored the adult as a child too, before nostalgia started setting in).

In this sense, the numerous different school editions still on sale of, say, *Gulliver's Travels* or *Robinson Crusoe* may be a better indication of adult insensitivity than children's enduring enthusiasm. But some classics do of course survive in a more active form: still read by children for pleasure rather than duty, and also lending themselves to TV, plays, films and even gramophone records or cassettes.

All five authors discussed in this section are still genuinely popular in this way, even though three of them began writing before the end of the century. They all share one significant characteristic: each author wrote his best-known book in conjunction with children, and without initial idea of publication. Toad's adventures had to be rescued from Kenneth Grahame's waste-paper basket; *The Hobbit* grew out of stories Tolkien told to his own children; *Peter Rabbit* began as an illustrated letter to a child friend; *Babar* started as a family story, later illustrated with drawings made by Jean de Brunhoff when separated from his sons by his own illness. *Little Black Sambo* was yet another story conveyed by letters, when Helen Bannerman was in India and again separated from her children.

Telling stories directly to children has always been a useful discipline to an author. An immediate audience soon makes its interest (or boredom) clear. Even when corresponding by letter, there must be a greater awareness of this audience than in writing for an impersonal public sometime in the future. Knowing a child well (and in writing letters, having little space to play with) may help an author get to the essence of what he has to say quickly and economically. Having no clear publication plans may release ideas and feelings an author might have second thoughts about in cold print. But once sanctified by the approval of an intimate audience of this sort, doubts may disappear. The result may be something close to the fantasy life of child and adult, both to an extent working upon the other as the story is being told.

The Wind in the Willows is perhaps one such book, and in the first extract, *The Children's Falstaff*, I try to unravel some of its great appeal in the blustering character of Toad. The use of talking animals in stories is as old as man himself, and found in folk-lore all over the world. As a literary device, talking animals also have many advantages to the author, remaining outside some of the pettifogging economic and social realities that often weigh down human characters. In both dreams and stories, animals can also stand for human passions, strengths and weaknesses that an audience may be happier in identifying elsewhere than in themselves. To this extent, the animal story can be an easy escape; in the hands of a master, from Aesop onwards, it can do much more.

Michael Wood specifically takes up the theme of escape in the next extract, *Tolkien's Fictions*. Merely avoiding immediate reality in fiction does not always imply running away from life. So-called mythopoeic writing, the legends, allegories and fantasies of man, may also reveal part of us to ourselves, something that might be missed in the sheer detail of contemporary, realistic writing. Imaginative, other-worldly writing, from George Macdonald to Tolkien, has often been segregated into a 'children's only' corner. Young people may of course be fascinated by it, but so also are many adults. The adventure story concentrating on bravery, the quest and the defeat of evil has always appealed, for reasons that may lie outside any precise contemporary parallels. For this reason, I doubt Michael Wood's explanation of *The Lord of the Ring* in terms of Smaug the dragon symbolising bombing raids in the second world war, and Sauron standing for Hitler. Other critics have suggested different parallels, with the horrors of trench warfare in the first world war, the nuclear waste-land, or the misery of a world destroyed by pollution. One of the functions of mythopoeic writing is to provide readers with a powerful imaginative framework around constant polarities, such as good versus evil, or domesticity versus the call of adventure. Within this framework, each generation can recognise its own particular preoccupations.

On a more domestic level, I have next chosen an article on Beatrix Potter. The tone here is hostile, but there should be no sacred cows – or rabbits – on any bookshelf, and although I don't agree with Mr Richardson, cogent criticism is more useful than the gushing appreciation that so often greets these little books. Personally, I am not convinced that Beatrix Potter only survives through adult nostalgia; her books have always been child-centred in a way few have ever rivalled. The small size, the sparse, action-packed text, with one picture a page, is perfectly adapted to small hands and smaller concentrations. The matter of the stories tends to run on well-proved lines of interest: temptation, danger, suspense, escape and retribution. The attraction of small, furry animals may possibly owe something to Freud, as Mr Richardson surmises, but there are more obvious explanations. Children too are small, cuddly and inexperienced in the ways of man. They also are perpetually curious, disobey parents, over-eat, are prone to fear, and suffer consequences. Naturally not all children will like these books, but for many they surely remain as relevant as ever, and there are no signs of their popularity diminishing.

The next piece, again by the admirably pugnacious Mr Richardson, concerns a political analysis of the early Babar books. *Teach your Baby to Rule* is clearly written tongue in cheek, but even so there are some important points made here. To the extent that literature has overt social values, it can often be said to carry a quite clear political message, and the Babar books are more political than most, clearly didactic over such matters as the welfare state, anti-militarism, and ordered democracy. How seriously we should take some of the other political values Mr Richardson reveals is another matter, but my guess is that this way of looking at children's literature may become more popular in the future, leading to a different type of literary debate, already seen in the controversy growing up around books like *Little Black Sambo*.

Up to now, Helen Bannerman's classic story has always been something of a favourite with parents and children, and the tone of Elizabeth Gard's article, *Bits strewn all over the Page*, an expanded radio interview with Helen Bannerman's daughter, is still basically friendly. Sambo, a jolly, resourceful little boy, is clearly the hero, and the whole story and scenery a charming example of Edwardian social attitudes. The objection, if any, might be to some of the violence, but Elizabeth Gard does not find that a serious criticism in her interesting article, although she has reservations about some other titles by the same author.

Janet Hill's angry and persuasive *Oh! Please Mr Tiger* was written only two years later, but already there had been a change affecting librarians, teachers and publishers everywhere. Scrutiny of children's literature for possibly undesirable views was growing again, sometimes reminiscent of the sort of concern Mrs Trimmer and her friends felt over different issues. To some extent, all this type of concern rests on fears of the possible effects of certain literature upon an audience, and perhaps there is better evidence now that so far as minority groups are concerned, people within them are offended and sometimes affected by attitudes and vocabulary others may not take so personally. Things can always change in this way; it would be silly, at the moment, to talk of banning the nursery rhyme 'Taffy was a Welshman', as there is little evidence of serious anti-Welsh prejudice anywhere. But verses like 'Ten little nigger boys', like the name Sambo itself, do offend, just as some of the Nazi pre-war anti-semitic picture books would offend if anyone tried reprinting them now. We pay a high price in human feeling if all possible social consequences of literature are persistently ignored, perhaps especially so far as children's literature is concerned.

But there remain many difficulties in all these arguments. What does Janet Hill mean when she says that *Little Black Sambo* should be consigned "to oblivion"? It is one thing to ban it from school or library shelf, but another to stop its sale altogether, possibly introducing another type of danger. Her article makes a useful starting point for what must always remain a very complex debate.

NICHOLAS TUCKER
The Children's Falstaff

Although *The Wind in the Willows* was written over sixty years ago, there are still no signs of its popularity waning with today's children and parents. It is now in its 105th edition, has a huge annual sale, and every Christmas A.A. Milne's adaptation *Toad of Toad Hall* is put on in the West End to full houses.

There are many enchanting things in this great work, but undoubtedly part of its continual fascination for children lies in the character and adventures of Toad. For Kenneth Grahame too, Toad was the first inspiration for the whole work. It is in letters to his son, Alastair, that we first hear stories about "this wicked animal", long before mention of the other river-bank characters. Although, of course, these early adventures of Toad were later absorbed into the main body of the book, they still stand virtually on their own in two of the main chapters, and certainly contain some of the funniest and most exciting episodes.

It says a great deal about children's reading tastes that they should so take to this "bad, low animal", in Grahame's own words, rather than to some of the more exalted characters that have appeared in children's books. In many ways, of course, Toad is the personification of the spoilt infant and is generally shown to glory in this, despite naggings from Badger and others. Adults who look to children's books for their generally improving qualities will find very little support in this character, which is perhaps why children enjoy him so. With his abundant flow of cash, Toad revels in his own omnipotence, buying house-boats, caravans and motor cars at will, just as in any childish fantasy, and for good measure steals on impulse as well. He is, as Piaget says of infants in general, in the classical egocentric stage; self-willed, boastful, unable to share the limelight, but basically insecure in strange situations, as in the fearful Wild Wood. He is a skilful liar too, but again, like so many infants, Toad seems almost to believe in his own fantasies, and perhaps cannot help treating the truth in such a relative way. When corrected, Toad can be quite genuinely sorry, but his sobs never last for very long, and cannot disguise his basic single-minded obstinacy. Indeed, this can result in the most violent infantile tantrums, where it takes two other animals to haul him upstairs to bed in disgrace, after having been rude and defiant to the stern parent-figure, Mr. Badger.

There is one especially interesting way in which Toad comes close to the hearts of today's children, and in a manner that Grahame could hardly have predicted. Toad was, perhaps, the first of the demon car drivers, or in his own phrases: "Toad the terror, the traffic-queller, the Lord of the lone trail, before whom all must give way or be smitten into nothingness and everlasting night." Children still warm to this fearful example far more than to any respectable puppet or policeman demonstrating the canons of road safety. Whatever the frightening statistics and the extra menace since Grahame's day, children's sympathies still seem to belong basically with the lawbreaker in this tragic field, and the following report from the *Belfast Telegraph*, although not recent, is still typical in this:

Over 1,000 Belfast school children were shown a series of films dealing with road safety in the Ritz cinema this moring. . . . The children's reactions to the pictures were worthy of note. They cheered the accidents, and laughed when an elderly cyclist wobbling over the road caused a collision ending in the death of one boy and the maiming of another.

Indeed, one can almost imagine Toad, with his seven smashes and three bouts in hospital under his belt, joining heartily in the fun.

Finally, of course, Toad renounces his old self, just as his audience one day will have to turn away from childhood. But typically, and consistent with Toad's almost irrepressible high spirits, this personal transformation is only wrung out of him extremely unwillingly after a final fling where Toad shows that he has no intention at all of learning any lessons from his previous bad behaviour.

Indeed, young readers sometimes wonder how long this change of personality is really going to last, and answering one such inquiry later on. Grahame himself wrote, "Of course Toad never really reformed; he was by nature incapable of it. But the subject is a painful one to pursue".

In his admirable biography, *Kenneth Grahame*, Peter Green traces the origin of Toad to Grahame's son, Alastair, along with touches of Horatio Bottomley and Oscar Wilde in Toad's penchant for loud clothes, after-dinner speaking and final downfall and imprisonment. There is also a certain ludicrous resemblance to the adventures and return of Ulysses. But there is surely another literary origin that must be mentioned, both in his likeness to Toad's actual shape and in his general effect upon the other characters. Grahame himself was for some time Honorary Secretary to the New Shakespeare Society, and Shakespeare was always one of his favourite authors: surely, when writing about Toad the image of Falstaff must have had some influence over him too. As it is, both characters have an intimate, although enforced, connexion with laundry, which finally results in their being thrown into the Thames. They each dress up as somebody else's aunt, and make a presentable, if finally unsuccessful, shot at passing off as an elderly lady. But more importantly, of course, through both of them runs the spirit of personified Riot, a perpetual and irrepressible threat to the status quo both of their friends and of the rather stuffy society outside that condemns them so freely. Falstaff torments the Lord Chief Justice, while Toad, never short of repartee, receives fifteen years' imprisonment for his "gross impertinence" to the rural police. Although Grahame described *The Wind in the Willows* as "Clean of the clash of sex", Toad alone has an eye for the women and takes it for granted that the Gaoler's daughter has fallen in love with him, in spite of the social gulf that also separates Falstaff from Doll Tearsheet. Toad's version of his escape from prison improves with each telling very much like Falstaff's Gadshill exploits, and while Falstaff is renounced at the end of the play, the riverbank animals renounce the old Toad, and the book itself goes on to assure us, as opposed to Grahame's letter quoted earlier, that the new Toad goes on to win the universal respect of all local inhabitants around him. Falstaff, in spite of or possibly because of what Tolstoy described as his "Gluttony, drunkenness, debauchery, rascality, deceit and cowardice", is probably Shakespeare's most popular comic character; Toad, that "dangerous and desperate fellow", has always been an especial favourite with children.

In fact, so far as adults were concerned, *The Wind in the Willows* had a cool reception to begin with, and was memorably condemned by *The Times,* which found that "As a contribution to natural history, the work is negligible". Opinion soon changed, however, often through the enthusiasm of children. The American President Theodore Roosevelt, for example, was persuaded by his family to give the book a second reading, and overcame his initial disappointment to become an enthusiastic convert. For children themselves, *The Wind in the Willows,* and especially the adventures of Toad, constituted one of those few books written not at them but for them. Toad himself was a character who dared do and express many of the things they may often have felt like doing, and such children could both feel superior to Toad's obvious deficiencies and excesses and also revel in them at the same time. With any amount of opportunity for moralizing, Grahame leaves the field mercifully clear to a few, largely unsuccessful efforts by the other riverbank animals to get Toad to mend his ways.

In fact, all the characters Grahame created are real and alive and in Toad he gave us a character who was even larger than life and in this sense, surely, becomes the children's Falstaff, whether Grahame consciously intended the connexion or not. We do not find in these pages any of those miserable creations who are merely the mouth-pieces for an adult's stereotyped vision of what is considered to be especially suitable for children. And in this, as in so many other things, *The Wind in the Willows* continues to be an object lesson for many of those who are writing for children today.

(From *The Times Literary Supplement,* June 26, 1969.)

MICHAEL WOOD
Tolkien's Fictions

George Eliot, for all her virtues, did a lot of damage to the novel. She drove out the demons that haunted Balzac and Dickens, depopulated their fanciful, animated worlds, and gave us a narrower, straighter notion of realism. She gave us, ultimately, Saul Bellow and Iris Murdoch: heavy feet on a small surface of already trampled ground.

But there is a new wind blowing. It comes from Buenos Aires, mainly: Borges. There is also Beckett, there is Nabokov. There are American writers like John Barth, Thomas Pynchon, Donald Barthelme, Richard Farina. Roughly, the assumption behind the work of all these people—echoed in the essays of Frank Kermode, who got it from Wallace Stevens—is that fiction is more than just a librarian's word for novels: a good deal of modern science, modern philosophy, indeed modern living (role playing, game playing) can be seen as the making of (helpful) fictions. Making fictions appears as primary human activity: language, say, being the first fiction. As soon as we have language, we can have stories, lies. We can say it's raining when it's not.

In this perspective, old-fashioned middle class realism begins to look rather limited, a poor use of the human imagination; and "realistic" SF of the kind Kingsley Amis admired, seems short-sighted and silly—an attempt to introduce George Eliot to Jules Verne, and have them write *Paradise Lost* together. Correspondingly, fantasy writers like Tolkien and Mervyn Peake may have to be moved in from the fringes of the recent literary scene.

I'm not thinking primarily of Tolkien's current vogue—his popularity among students, the incredible sales of his work in

America, the coffee bars called Middle Earth, or the doctoral dissertations comparing him with St Augustine. All that belongs to a vaster, vaguer problem: our general lack of spiritual funds, which has thrown up gurus stranger than Tolkien. It is certainly true that straight fiction speaks little enough to our wider worries.

But my concern here is with something else. Realism in the narrow sense is not a neutral word. The suggestion behind it is not only that the "real world" is like this, but that we have no business to be fooling with fanciful alternatives. Acceptance of "reality" is a cardinal virtue. A person who says he dislikes fantasy, usually doesn't like the idea of the imagination at play. He dislikes the idea of *escape*, which he tends to equate—as Tolkien says in a lecture on fairy stories—with desertion. He sees the world as a liberal republic, not as a prison. He is inviting us to work towards progress within the system, and not cop out into what he thinks of as sentimentality. This is the voice of George Eliot or Ruskin objecting to Dickens. It is a view which wipes out epic, romance and tragedy; and the prevalence of the view is the reason why we have none of those things except in ashamed or embarrassed or freakish forms.

Fantasy, then, is a form of opposition to the democratic and scientific world-picture which flourished in the 19th century—hence its frequently fascist or antiquarian streak. But it has its radical aspects too, which I'll classify crudely as metaphysical, moral and visionary.

That is, first, fantasy may question the prevailing world-picture itself. Its fantastic alternatives may serve to make us wonder how fantastic our own notions of reality are. Borges works very much in this way. Secondly, fantasy may ask what reality *should* be like. It works then as satire or speculation, as in Plato or Swift, or in good science fiction. And thirdly, fantasy can offer more or less credible alternatives to what we think of as the real world. In this category there would obviously be utopias, like those of More, Rabelais and Bacon; but, more to my point, there would also be works which offered, not a social or legislative programme but simply new forms or contexts for human behaviour—applications of tolerance, courage or intelligence, for example—which might have some relevance to the world we live in. Mervyn Peake succeeds here, and so does John Brunner, a science fiction writer, in *The Long Result*. Tolkien doesn't, although he scores fairly well in the other categories. The categories are not really separable—they run in and out of each other constantly.

In 1937, Tolkien published *The Hobbit*, a children's classic on a level with *Pooh* and *The Wind in the Willows*. Hobbits are peaceful, beer-loving, pipe-smoking creatures with furry feet who live in holes in the ground—a cross between moles and Oxford dons. Bilbo Baggins, a braver hobbit than most, goes off with some dwarves in search of dragon's treasure, and after many adventures, comes home loaded with booty: the dragon is dead, and the dwarves have been restored to their ancestral home under the distant mountain. Bilbo also found a ring, which is the link between this earlier book and the grandiose trilogy called *The Lord of the Rings*, published in 1954 and 1955, and written between 1936 and 1949.

The ring, it turns out, is a master ring forged by the evil Sauron and taken from him at the end of an earlier world war. The conquerors of Sauron lost it, and the ring, after slipping from several hands in the attempt to get back to its lord, came to Bilbo. Sauron now knows that the ring is in the Shire, the cosy homeland of the hobbits, and is trying to recover it. If he succeeds, the whole world will fall under his dark dominion.

The story of *The Lord of the Rings* is the story of the quest of Frodo, Bilbo's hobbit-heir, aided by Gandalf, a wizard, and a group of trusty companions—two men, an elf, a dwarf and some more hobbits—to destroy the ring before it can return to Sauron. The quest, after some 1,300 pages, ends. The ring is cast into the fire-mountain, and the rule of darkness is staved off, at least temporarily. Only temporarily, because Sauron himself, we are told, is "but a servant or emissary" of some other, larger, more permanent force of evil. Just as, we suspect, the good wizard and the elves are instruments of God.

Tolkien is a Catholic and an Anglo-Saxon scholar, and the theology of his work is an extraordinary synthesis of heroic northern myth and Christian promise. Tolkien believes in Providence, both in and out of his fiction. He never mentions chance without a pious parenthesis—"if such it be"—yet he also believes, as he suggests the author of *Beowulf* believed, that within Time the monsters win. "We have fought the long defeat," Tolkien's Elf-Queen says, and the elves effectively leave the earth. God, in other words, is pulling his punches, to see how we make out against Sauron and his ilk. The treats come later, in the islands of the blessed.

This view accounts, I think, for two things in Tolkien's work. First, the fascination with the journey—not only in *The Hobbit* and *The Lord of the Rings* passim, but also in the rather thin stories, *Leaf by Niggle* and *Smith of Wootton Major*; the journey becomes a figure or type of death, the happy release, the blessed departure. And secondly, the elegiac tone of the trilogy, which seems strangely at odds with its heroic theme. Tolkien, lecturing on *Beowulf* to the British Academy in 1936, found the same double strain in the old epic—"an heroic-elegiac poem," he called it, "a poem by a learned man writing of old times." Both descriptions fit Tolkien and his fiction so perfectly that one wonders whether he was not writing his own programme for the next 13 years.

Tolkien's "old times" are only half-mythical. They are a magical Arthurian past, certainly; a lost age where lords and ladies dally sweetly on the greensward and talk like Tennyson, where elves and dwarves and hobbits and wizards and other, older creatures are available for chats with mortal men. It is a haunted world where trees move and mountains threaten and the weather is always a metaphor—a world where at least one of what Tolkien calls "primordial human desires" is satisfied: the desire to "hold communion with other living things." It is an elvish Eden, a world seen in the

morning, when "al was this land fulfild of fayerye," as the
Wife of Bath put it. But Tolkien's old times are also simply
historical, a picture of pre-industrial England, a place of un-
spoiled greenery, fields and forests. Forests especially.

Tolkien writes beautifully about trees—largely, I suspect,
because he prefers them to people. At the end of the trilogy,
when the quest is over, the heroic hobbits return to the
Shire to find that Sauron's agents have been busy there too.
There are chimneys belching out black smoke, and mean
houses have replaced the picturesque burrows. There is arbi-
trary imprisonment, and there are distinct unfairnesses in the
distribution of beer and tobacco. It's a tame picture of the
great darkness: a mingling of a dim view of socialism and a
wishful view of Hitler's Germany.

What is there, then, in this Tory daydream to prevent it
from being the mishmash that Edmund Wilson thought it
was? Why would people like Richard Hughes, Naomi Mitchi-
son and C.S. Lewis want to compare Tolkien with Spenser,
Malory and Ariosto (respectively)? The answer lies less, I
think, in the quality or texture of Tolkien's work than in the
extent and variety of it, and in the power of the complex
moral fable which he manages to sustain.

Tolkien's borrowings are considerable: lines from heroic
lays, a horn from Roland, an interesting case of resurrection
from *The Golden Bough*, and a swan from an expensive
staging of *Lohengrin*. Some of his "sources" are less dignified.
The Orcs and Southrons in the pay of Sauron all look like
Japs or Arabs: dark skins, slant eyes and scimitars. Smaug,
the dragon in *The Hobbit*, floating down the wind "like a
monstrous crow," attacking the town on the lake from the
air, is a bombing raid from the second world war. And this
description of the hobbits—a "curiously tough" people—must
surely strike a chord in loyal hearts? ". . . they were, perhaps,
so unwearyingly fond of good things not least because they
could, when put to it, do without them, and could survive
rough handling by grief, foe, or weather in a way that aston-
ished those who did not know them well and looked

no further than their bellies and their well-fed faces."

Saruman, the wizard who goes bad, is a version of the mad scientist of the thirties "But we must have power, power to order all things as we will . . ." and Gandalf, the good wizard, whistles for his faithful horse like Roy Rogers. And then, where did you hear this dialect before, which is spoken in *The Lord of the Rings* by the helpful Wild Men of the Woods? "Wild Men have long ears and eyes; know all paths. Wild Men live here before Stonehouses; before Tall Men come up out of Water . . ." Heap good writing.

But I don't intend these remarks as a criticism of Tolkien—well, only partly. They also give an idea of his range, which is wider than it looks. So that although he is capable of all kinds of archaic awfulness ("Rede oft is found at the rising of the Sun"), he is also capable of this characterisation of Sauron's evil eye, seen in an elf-mirror: "The Eye was rimmed with fire, but was itself glazed, yellow as a cat's, watchful and intent, and the black slit of its pupil opened on a pit, a window into nothing." Roughly, Tolkien is good when the action is moving, and embarrassing when it stops. He is a born story-teller and a bad writer. The battle between Gandalf and the Balrog, for example, an ancient evil awakened from its long sleep under the mountain, is as exciting as anything since *Moby Dick*, but the halt in Lorien, the land of the elves, is more like Maurice Hewlett or Anthony Hope.

Tolkien was born in 1892 (Nabokov and Borges were both born in 1899), but he belongs to an older generation: that of Yeats and the friends of Madame Blavatsky. The enemy is science, or rather the complacency of science, the self-satisfaction of people who think they can explain everything, who have no time for myths, for forms of truth which will not fit within a narrow rationalism. Hence Tolkien's fantasy, his insistence on the *possibility* of "fayerye"; hence Yeats's flirtations with the occult. Frodo the hobbit "looked at maps, and wondered what lay beyond their edges."

This is the striking thing about Tolkien's imagined world: the precision of its geography, the colour of the map beyond the map's edges. Tolkien is not good at creating individuals, but his types, his races, are fascinating. There are dwarves, orcs, elves, hobbits, ents, men, dragons, wizards, trolls, goblins, ghosts, all sharply differentiated, all speaking their own dialects. Dwarves, for example, are decent, greedy, gold-loving folk, good at metalwork and fond of caves. Ents are animated trees, slow-talking, slow-moving creatures older than almost anything else on earth. Wizards are quaint and stuffy, and the men are a craggy, grey-eyed, heroic and thoroughly boring lot. The hobbits are sentimentalised by Tolkien, but still attractive. Dragons are tricky, but polite.

But all this still sounds closer to *The Wizard of Oz* than to Ariosto. What else is there? First, there is Tolkien's unrelenting psychologism. There are heroic adventures here, but they are all carefully internalised. The authentic acts of courage — a hobbit deciding to face a dragon, a handful of men deciding to fight against all odds — always take place in the mind. And the authentic conflicts of the trilogy are always telepathic — clashes of wills, combats of concentration. Good and evil are thus not abstractions, they are a confrontation. They are congregations of like-minded creatures lined up in opposition. The recruiting and the battles and the weather are simply metaphors for this.

And then the conflict in any case is not a simple one. The ring which Frodo has to destroy is a ring of power. If Sauron gets it back, nothing will be safe from him. But why shouldn't an enemy of Sauron use it against him, for the good of the world? This is the argument and the temptation offered to several important characters. The answer is that the ring simply is evil. Anyone who tried to use it would either become a servant of Sauron, or if he were very strong, become Sauron himself, a new dark lord. There is no good in the ring, no way of using it well.

Tolkien has said that his work is not an allegory, and it isn't, in any narrow sense. But it certainly isn't just a jolly tale either, and the rings represents something, whether Tolkien knows what it is or not. Ultimately, the ring represents the lure of the modern world itself, which must stain all those who try to change it or use it. "The blood-dimmed tide is loosed," as Yeats wrote, and the only answer is high conservatism: war without compromise, and without resort to the engines of the enemy. This is the long defeat the Elf-Queen spoke of, because a modern war on those terms cannot be won. But Tolkien would say, I think, that the war cannot be won anyway, and that the alternatives are death with clean or with dirty hands. The model is a desperate, noble wager which works in romance and inevitably fails in real life.

I don't find this an attractive or a realistic position, but I think it is a powerful and a coherent one—it is the position of Swift and Pope faced with what they saw as the rising darkness—and I think it has a lot to do with Tolkien's success, whether with poets or writers or students or teachers or hippies. "The world withers," Tolkien writes in an alliterating poem based on *The Battle of Maldon*, "and the wind rises;/ the candles are quenched. Cold falls the night." *Beowulf,* anyone?

(From *New Society*, March 27, 1969).

PATRICK RICHARDSON
Miss Potter and the Little Rubbish

When did Beatrix Potter die? Worshippers will not stop this side of immortality; a psychologist might say 1913, the year she married a Lake District solicitor, when the flow of nursery books virtually dried up; the prosaic answer is 23 December 1943. She was 77 years old, and this is her centenary.

So here we go. An exhibition is to be mounted at the National Book League (the press hand-out says bravely, "Few writers can vie with the reputation of Beatrix Potter . . ."), the Tate Gallery has the originals of the illustrations for *The Tailor of Gloucester*, and the Queen bought the manuscript. Whatever came over the Postmaster General that a centenary series of postage stamps was not issued? Think of the success of the 4d Peter Rabbit Blue, with a McGregor Brown as an alternative for Scotland.

But what are we celebrating? Beatrix Potter wrote 19 children's stories between 1902 and 1913. The books were illustrated with her own pastel paintings. Most of these have remained in print in their original format ever since, and must be pillars of Fredk Warne, Miss Potter's publishers, quite apart from the industrial complex of toys, games, ornaments, crockery and wallpaper that has grown from the first appearance of the books.

How good are the books? As children's books they must clearly be judged by particular standards of communication to their audience, and in this respect there is little doubt that they succeed. However, higher claims have been made for them as literature. Graham Greene wrote a scintillating essay on the Potter books, in which he found the way in which she

173

"puts aside love and death with a gentle detachment reminiscent of Mr E.M. Forster," and felt that in Peter Rabbit and Benjamin Bunny the author had "created two epic personalities," and that "there are few fights in literature which can compare in excitement with the duel between Mr Tod and Tommy Brock."

This was an elaborate and amusing exercise, dismissed by Miss Potter out of hand as an example of the Freudian school of criticism, and it certainly misses the point. So far the books have shown staying power, but this stems from their strong nostalgic appeal rather than their literary merit.

This nostalgia is evoked from the combination of the pictures and the text. The stories alone are rather thin, while the little pastel pictures have been ludicrously over-rated. To talk of them as being in the tradition of Constable (Margaret Lane) or Samuel Palmer (Janet Adam Smith in *The Listener*) is clearly ridiculous. It was one of the more endearing Potter characteristics that she too found this "absolute bosh, rubbish." At their very best the pictures have some affinities with the Pre-Raphaelites, although lacking their clearly defined aims and values.

The pictures belong squarely in the tradition of the little watercolours that so many Victorian and Edwardian amateurs made on their holidays.

But what of the goings-on in these landscapes and fussy interiors? It is at this point that the difficulties begin. The Potter technique was to draw animals—"the little rubbish, like mice and rabbits—dogs and sheep and horses are on a higher level"—from the life or death, even dressing her models in a costume suitable to their required character. The animals are done with great care, but without imagination. "I can't invent," wrote Beatrix, "I only copy."

The effect is almost exactly that of the elaborate taxidermy beloved of the Victorians, and surviving best in that remarkable relic, the Mouse Museum at Bramber in Sussex (the work of a William Potter by a sensational coincidence—but unluckily no relation of Beatrix). There the kittens, rabbits, rats and mice reconstruct the whole social scene of the period. The effect of the Bramber set-pieces is quite nauseating, and there is something of this in the books. The dignity of the animals—such as it is—is dissipated.

But the very efficiency of the animal drawings prevents any real development of character, which is essential if the animals are meant to be "little people," as they clearly are from the texts. The rabbits and mice are never more than mere rabbits and mice. We only get their imposed characteristics from the cleverly chosen costumes. Thus no one can tell Peter Rabbit without clothes from Benjamin or any other Potter rabbit; the squirrels in *Squirrel Nutkin* are indistinguishable.

Nor does their conversation or the text help the development of character much. Aunt Beatrix speaks for them all; they use her vocabulary—"I am affronted"; "soporific"; "improvident"; "doleful"; "implored him to exert himself."

As the subjects become more complex, so the books grind to a halt. The Potter people are impossibly bad. One is convinced that Beatrix Potter did not understand people, and possibly had never made a close study of them. Lucie in *Mrs Tiggy Winkle* is a doll, living and partly living. It is revealing that the one memorable character in any of the books is Mr McGregor, who is drawn impressionistically from a superb original once seen briefly by the author "extended full length on his stomach weeding a carriage drive with a knife."

What are the themes of the books? There is undoubtedly a pursuit theme, and this is an important contact with children, Jemima Puddleduck's whole story is a pursuit by a fox. The stories have a strength in that they do not dodge the facts of death, although of course it is not something that happens to the main characters.

Secondly, there is an obsession with cleanliness. In nearly every story there are long accounts of ruthless cleaning operations—of clothes, children, or houses. Some stories— such as *Mrs Tiggy Winkle* and *Tom Kitten* are about nothing else. In a letter to her publisher the author went to great trouble to emphasise this obsession. "She [Mrs Tiggy Winkle] is supposed to be exorcising spots and iron stains, same as Lady Macbeth . . ."

Then there is the insistence on the procedures of etiquette that make the books period pieces and give them much of their adult appeal. We read of "the dignity and repose" of a tea party, and in *The Pie and the Patty Pan* we have the full account of the invitation, the greeting at the door and the formalities at table.

There are two major attitudes in the books that have made them important influences as nursery literature, as opposed to children's books. These are the twin upperclass (and bourgeois by short-range assimilation) attitudes towards animals— that one loves them but that they are also killed—and towards the concept of a hierarchical system in society—that there are gardeners and washerwomen in the natural order of things. This latter was clearly true in Miss Potter's day when it would have been unexceptionable, but now it can only implant or reinforce an anachronistic view of society at an early age.

The books hardly deserve the paraphernalia of a centenary. They lack the wit and imagination of Lewis Carroll, the characterisation of A.A. Milne, and the social observation to be found in Kenneth Grahame. They fill a tiny niche in the child's bookshelf. They are short, simple and suitable for the first attempts at reading to an infant.

But if the books are not outstanding, the career of the author is a fascinating example of the upbringing and attitudes of a woman of her class and period. The maiden aunt is an English phenomenon, tragic and wasted. Only the chance success of the first privately printed edition of *Peter Rabbit* enabled Beatrix Potter to escape this fate.

Born in 1866, she suffered the upbringing of a well-to-do child. Her life at the daily and at the yearly levels was almost completely routine. Her parents had inherited considerable wealth, ironically from robust, self-made Lancashire industrialists. Her father, trained for law, made a life's work of doing nothing, while her mother concentrated on shielding Beatrix from any taint of commerce or industry. The pressures exerted on the girl were enormous—she refers to "such painful unpleasantness at home" when she was 40.

Her early life was starved of affection, and she was clearly emotionally retarded. This is shown by her mania for collecting animals—either dead for stuffing or alive for companionship. There was a real Peter Rabbit, a real Hunca Munca and a real Mrs Tiggy.

It was from this emotional "set" that the stories grew, spontaneously enough in letters to begin with, then carefully developed after her failure to be accepted as a botanical illustrator. "I have just made stories to please myself, because I never grew up."

The stories became the whole of her life for a while. She became fascinated by the technical and business sides of their publication, became deeply involved with the charming family of her publisher, and finally became engaged to their son, who unfortunately died in 1905. "Publishing books," she wrote in defence of her daring action, "is as clean a trade as spinning cotton."

Partly to avoid this emotional crisis, and because she now had some money, Beatrix Potter bought a farm in the Lake District, and concentrated on producing books—13 in eight years. Her books and her farming at last allowed her to unleash some of her energies. They also account for a hilarious entry into the 1910 general election. She campaigned for the Tory Party's policy of Protection, in her case to stop cheap dolls from Germany underselling her home-produced products. The pamphlet outlining the fate of "poor Camberwell Dolly" ends up with the Lady Bountiful cry, "It is uphill work, trying to help folk who will not help themselves. Why should *I* bother myself about the British workman, if he prefers Free Trade?"

In 1913 the flow of books dried up, except for a few disastrous later efforts winkled out of her by the Americans. In that year Beatrix Potter, then aged 47, married her solicitor.

At last the maiden aunt had made the full transition from her latter-day Victorian cocoon to womanhood. It is revealing that her sublimation in her books ceased at once. Her long life was now centred on preserving the Lake District, often by bequests to the National Trust, and on building up an indigenous Lake District breed of sheep. Desperately, often rudely, she rebuffed admirers of Beatrix Potter and insisted always on being Mrs Heelis, farmer. "I object" she wrote "to being supposed to be the wife of Sidney Webb, a member of the late Socialist government. He married a Miss Beatrice Potter—no relation."

So why the centenary? It may seem to be a tribal rite of the British grand bourgeoisie celebrating their nursery culture, exulting in a paean of praise to the recorder of their ideal, uncomplicated world. But one must be very, very wary about any such conclusion. It is only a week since the BBC was inundated with outraged telephone calls from people objecting to the idea of using hedgehogs as croquet balls in *Alice in Wonderland.* Not a word however for the flamingo mallets, who would seem to have the more painful part to play.

Freud has shown the significance of the appeal of soft, furry creatures. By accident Beatrix Potter tapped this rich vein. And the appeal is by no means dead. The spokesman against all that Beatrix Potter stood for during her creative period must be Jimmy Porter. And how is he when we last see him? Kneeling on the floor with his wife, the "angry young man" says: "We'll be together in our bear's cave, and our squirrel's drey, and we'll live on honey, and nuts—lots and lots of nuts . . . And I'll see that you keep that sleek, bushy tail glistening as it should, because you're a very beautiful squirrel, but you're none too bright either, so we've got to be careful. There are cruel, steel traps lying about everywhere, just waiting for rather mad, slightly satanic, and very timid little animals. Poor squirrels!"

If this is the voice of the Great Non-Conformist, then Miss Potter should be good for the next 100 years at least.

(From *New Society,* July 7, 1966).

* John Osborne, *Look Back in Anger* (Faber 1957).

Teach your Baby to Rule

Edmund Leach has analysed Babar the elephant's carefully constructed world (*New Society*, 20 December 1962), and there is no doubt that this cohesion gives the books much of their adult satisfaction. But the earlier Babar stories have much more to offer: they are a primer in power politics.

In the first of his key books, *The Story of Babar*, Jean de Brunhoff described a do-it-yourself *coup d'état*. Babar is born into a primitive, matriarchal, child-centred community, which has no defined economic system and is ruled by a monarch chosen by the elders and elected by acclamation.

Babar himself left this society—its primitiveness is stressed by the nakedness of its members—and went to the west, where he was educated and made lasting contacts with capitalist elements, represented in the books by the "very rich Old Lady," who "gave him everything he wanted."

The mechanism of the plot is left implicit. Arthur and Celeste, two cousins of Babar—they are still naked, unlike Babar himself who is now dressed in the height of western fashion—race into town, where they too are bought clothes. Their haste is not explained in the book, except by the sinister coincidence ("Alas! That very day . . .") of the King of the Elephants dying of poison. Babar makes rapid preparations to return to his country, while Cornelius, his future chief minister, arranges the election procedure, timing it to coincide with Babar's sensational return ("Just at that moment . . .") in a motor car, representing western technology.

Cornelius played his part "in his quavering voice," a defect that is significantly never mentioned again. "My dear friends, we must have a new king . . . Why not choose Babar?" And, although Babar has been out of the country since childhood, his election is stampeded through the bewildered "electors".

Cornelius is quickly rewarded for his part ("You have such good ideas I shall make you a general"), and is given a hat to mark his elevation to the power group. The later emphasis in the story on this hat can only be explained by its significance as a symbol of power. A Royal Wedding—Babar has conveniently become engaged to Celeste "on our journey in the car"—is immediately staged further to seduce the population and to persuade neighbouring powers to recognise the new regime.

The second book, *Babar's Travels*, shows the establishment of his position as the result of a rather specious military success. Babar had begun his reign in a surprising way by setting off for his honeymoon in a balloon. Undoubtedly the real reason for this trip to the west was to reestablish contact with western capitalists and to raise support for his government.

His account of his travels is so patently incredible that one can only conclude that it was invented for publicity purposes for a childlike people. In any event Babar returns to the scene of a war in his country with the Old Lady herself, on this occasion in an aeroplane, symbolising an even more sophisticated technology. He quickly wins a battle by an imaginative but unheroic trick that nevertheless establishes him as a "great general." His primitive, still naked people are treated to a victory celebration, which features certain rewards for the Old Lady (mineral resources?) for extremely vaguely defined services rendered. (She had "been so kind to them . . .") the power group of Babar, Queen Celeste, cousin Arthur, the Old Lady, Cornelius and a foreign favourite "Babar's friend Zephir" (a monkey) is now complete.

In the third Jean de Brunhoff story, *Babar the King*, Babar digs in. Characteristically, he establishes a new city, Celeste-ville. This turns out to be an unimaginatively planned city with rows of identical houses, rising up to the juxtaposed Orwellian Palaces of Work and Pleasure, flanked by the large houses of Babar and the Old Lady. There is no opposition to this project. (" 'Hear, hear' cried the elephants, raising their trunks in the air" —clearly a fascist salute.)

Any criticism is silenced by the timely arrival of loads of foreign luxury consumer goods ("dresses, hats, silks, paint boxes, drums, tins of peaches, feathers, racquets . . ."). The existing inhabitants are persuaded off the site by another Orwellian ploy of a parrot claque chanting: "Come and see Celesteville, most beautiful of towns." To convince his people of their emergence as a power, all are now given clothes, hitherto the prerogative of the ruling group. A national anthem, incomprehensible to all, is produced by Cornelius as "The Old Song of The Mammoths," and this is sung by a specially rehearsed children's choir.

Socially a lot is made of a sort of Owenite idea of the equality of labour, but this very rapidly develops into a privileged hierarchy on the one side and uniformed gardeners and cooks on the other. Babar significantly plays tennis with Pilophage, a general, while the intellectuals form a bowls clique. The theatre becomes the social apex with ludicrously full evening dress worn for what appears to be Molière. Nothing could be more alien to this primitive people.

After a year another of the huge non-events is staged—this one being to commemorate the founding of the city, which is to be celebrated by a May Day type parade. The workers are marched past in their gaudy fancy dresses, while one notices that in only a year a powerful military element has appeared, both in the parade in their elite uniforms and lining the route. Babar has developed his personality cult to the extent of sitting on a mechanical horse.

Towards the end of this book one of the great mysteries of the saga occurs. Both Cornelius, who paved the way for Babar's accession, and the Old Lady, who financed it, are victims of simultaneous "accidents," on both occasions in the presence of Babar or the Court group. Ironically Babar's efficient hospital and fire services save both victims, and some sort of *rapprochement* is reached in the grounds of the hospital. The humourless Babar tries to explain this setback to his bid for sole power in terms of a mystical dream, hurriedly producing a rather unpolished new bromide: "Let us work and play with a will and we shall always be happy."

In the last of the mainstream books, *Babar at Home*, we see the system fully operative, and Babar a conservative father figure. Babar and Celeste are anxious for an heir—they in fact produce triplets—as the dictatorship is to be made permanent by transformation into a hereditary monarchy. The babies wear baby crowns in some pictures. A proclamation for the happy event is made by the army. (Drums; and the people "running up in great numbers listened respectfully.") The arrivals are announced by gun salutes fired by the King's Artillery in the Fort of St John, which has mysteriously appeared to dominate Celesteville. Soldiers are now a common sight on the roads.

The whole book deals with the problems of raising the heirs safely, since they have become essential to the survival of the dynasty. As Babar says frankly to Celeste, "I don't know what we should do without them."

The political substructure of the story is as pointed as that in *Animal Farm*, with perhaps a higher degree of universality. The whole machinery of dictatorship is here: the capitalist-backed coup, the nationalist trimmings, the deception of the people by status symbols, the reality of military backing and the inner power struggles. The entire system is secured by a carefully developed personality cult of omniscience, justice and kindness. Brunhoff wrote these books in the 1930s, and his Babar is surely a parody reaction to the peculiar political climate in France and Europe at the time. Leach attributed some of the appeal of these books to adults to their prophetic powers. General Charles may well be the French mass's wish-fulfilment for a Babar.

The books ·now republished are not fundamental to the epic. Jean de Brunhoff's *Babar's Friend Zephir* is at least a fringe statement. It sees Babar's state beginning to push its own ideology out to a more primitive neighbour, just as

Babar himself was a product of the west. But even in the monkey state the social structure is carefully observed and the military power structure is immediately interesting. But even Jean de Brunhoff may have worked out true Babar vein — *Babar and Father Christmas* (also due for reissue) has little further to offer. The books by the younger Laurence de Brunhoff merely use Babar as a cuddly nursery figure in two fairly charming but empty little tales. They really have nothing to do with the main statement.

(From *New Society*, March 10, 1966).

ELIZABETH GARD
Bits strewn all over the Page

When my son passed the ABC, nursery-rhyme, stage, and began to need *real stories*, I was gratified, as I expect many other parents have been, to find so many of the familiar books of my own childhood still available and popular. Peter Rabbit, Babar, and even Christopher Robin, seem to be holding their own against the lavishly illustrated, sensitively-written productions which are published by the hundred every year. But the most enjoyable rediscovery for me – the books which have come best through the second-time-around test – have been Helen Bannerman's *Little Black Sambo*, and his successors, *Little Black Mingo, Quibba, Quasha and Bobtail.*

Little Black Sambo is one of the most successful books ever written for the two-to-five age-group. It sells an average of 25,000 copies a year, and the others aren't far behind. The more I read them to my own and other children, and the more I discuss them with other adults, the more convinced I am that their success owes more to the enthusiasm of *children* than their parents.

Some children's classics, Christopher Robin certainly, and perhaps even some of Beatrix Potter's mild little pastel creatures, I suspect are persistently offered to children by sentimental adults who probably didn't enjoy them all that much when they were at the receiving end. Whereas with the Little Black books, I think it's the other way round – children keep on asking for·them, but adults often shy away from them. There's a certain amount of to my mind rather ludicrous, liberal unease about the portrayal of 'little blacks'. Also, even parents who take the modern view that children should not be too protected, often recoil from the savagery of the stories. It was this unease I encountered which first aroused my curiosity about Helen Bannerman. Compared to Beatrix Potter, or even Enid Blyton, she seemed an unaccountably unknown figure.

The only clue on the title page was — "First Published 1899". That confirmed my original guess that she was part of the British Raj. The vocabulary gives her away — words like bazaar, chatty, mugger, and ghi (the melted tiger butter). But the setting is a puzzling jumble. The vegetation is tropical jungle, but the mud-hut villages look completely African. The animals are all Indian, but the humans look as if they've come straight off the plantation. They have the clothes and the features of Southern States cotton-pickin' Negroes.

My first guess turned out to be right. Helen Bannerman lived for thirty years in India. She was born and brought up in Edinburgh, took a university degree (a rare achievement for a woman in those days), and married a fellow Scot, William Burney Bannerman, a doctor in the Indian Medical Service, who ended up Surgeon-General in the Indian Army.

The Bannermans led very much the conventional life of British people in India. They travelled about with their entourage of servants, mainly in Bombay and Madras. Nothing particularly exciting seems to have happened to her. She herself had had none of the hair-raising encounters with fearsome beasts that she described so convincingly in her books — (Though on her way out there she had been made to hide behind a tree while the bullocks which were pulling the wagon were changed, lest a sight so strange as a white woman might make them bolt.) But in her approach to the job of entertaining and amusing her children, Mrs. Bannerman was far from conventional. She made up her own stories and drew her own pictures. Her daughter, Dr. Davie Bannerman, had kept a marvellous collection of letters from her mother, written in a clear script and illustrated with engaging ink and watercolour sketches. (She could draw Indians beautifully when she wanted to.) Dr. Bannerman also remembers how

Little Black Sambo came to be written and published:

Dr. Bannerman: My mother when she was a small child had always wanted a little book that was small enough to hold in her own hands, because she'd been often ticked off for not handling books carefully enough, and she wanted a little book that had the picture and the letterpress on opposite pages, so that she didn't have to look forwards and backwards and I think it was with the idea of realising this ambition for my sister and me that she originally made *Little Black Sambo* into a book. She just wrote them – the first one anyway – for my sister and me. We had been left alone, at least without our parents, in the hills because it was considered more healthy and children were very apt to die off in India at that time if they were kept too much in the plains. And so we were no doubt missing her, and she made this little book to sort of comfort us (she just bound it by hand and sent it to us in the hills.)

Interviewer: And was she surprised at its success?

Dr. Bannerman: Yes, I think she was. I don't think she would have expected it to catch on really at all, especially when all the publishers refused it to begin with.

Interviewer: Who suggested to her that they should be published?

Dr. Bannerman: She was somebody who visited our house and she and her husband were going home on leave, and she said she thought it ought to be published, and my mother was a bit doubtful whether anybody would want it, but she said 'Let me have the manuscript to take home with me,' and she went round the various publishing houses to see if she could get it taken on.

Interviewer: And her subsequent books?

Dr. Bannerman: Her subsequent books got in quite easily because as soon as *Little Black Sambo* had been a success, you see, the publishers were quite willing to have the later ones. The later ones brought in a great deal more money because the copyright had to be sold of Black Sambo before it was published, but he opened the door for the later books.

Elizabeth Gard:

It's not difficult to see why *Little Black Sambo* has always been the favourite. The story is simpler and less gruesome than in the later books — yet it is eventful enough. Each picture exactly illustrates a moment in the story. There is none of the self-indulgence one finds in so many modern children's books, where a whimsical insubstantial text wisps around illustrations of great beauty but little narrative point. The simple words, and the highly effective repetition — each tiger growling identically "Little Black Sambo, I'm going to eat you up" rivet the attention of both reader and listener. Mrs. Bannerman seems to have fallen completely instinctively into just the right style for children.

Dr. Bannerman: Well, of course, she was accustomed to talking to us children in language that we could understand, and I suppose that made it so that other children could too.

Interviewer: But if you compare them with other children's books of that period, at the turn of the century, even Beatrix Potter contains a lot of words which children didn't understand, and which obviously she realised they wouldn't, like 'soporific' and words like this that your mother always seems to avoid.

Dr. Bannerman: Well, my mother always tried to avoid writing for grown-ups; she said she was quite aware that grown-ups prefer other pastel colours and that sort of thing but that she had found that children liked bright and garish colours, and so she always painted the pictures to suit the children and not to catch the eye of the grown-ups. And I suppose it was the same with the wording of it.

Elizabeth Gard:

There's another important aspect in which I find Helen Bannerman's books are instinctively well judged, perfectly attuned to children's needs. They are all frightening — not frightening enough to upset or disturb children, but just frightening enough to excite them. One recurrent theme is the devouring of small and helpless creatures by large and savage beasts. The books are full of threatened and actual gobblings, and miraculous regurgitations.

There are one or two really violent episodes. In *Little Black Quasha* the tigers fight to the death over the right to eat her up. "Ears and tails were flying through the air, hair and blood were strewn upon the ground" — and strewn upon the printed page. In *Little Black Mingo*, the baleful crocodile (the old Mugger) swallows the cruel old woman Black Noggy, and the kerosene and matches she is carrying. The kerosene explodes inside the Mugger's 'dark inside' and both the wicked characters are blown into little bits. (All the wicked characters in these books end up in little bits). And there in the following illustration are all the gory fragments spattered across the page. In the last picture, Mingo and her friend the mongoose, without any sign of squeamishness, are sitting on the Mugger's fearsome head, having a cup of tea. David Holbrook, a well-known educationalist, considers it "a shattering story; Timon of Athens for toddlers", but advises parents not to flinch from it.

I agree with him. In my experience children relish a certain amount of gruesome detail. Savage instincts and frightening fantasies are already there in the child's imagination. Games about giants, witches and tigers, and stories like these, help to release and contain their fantasies. They also help children to place the violence they are more or less bound to see on television. And *Little Black Mingo* is nothing like, say, '*Struwwelpeter*' or *The Tinder Box*. The innocent and helpless always escape, and the violence is confined to the animal world.

But Helen Bannerman did write one book, not now available, which I wouldn't want to show my children. Called *Little Kettle Head*, it is about a little girl (a little white girl), who pulls a pan of boiling water down from the stove, and has her head burnt off. A kind Indian servant makes her a new wooden head and fixes it to her truncated neck. "But she doesn't like it, and she cries and cries." That night as she lies miserably in bed, her own dear little head is miraculously returned to her. There it lies on a chair, with its fair hair

spread out, and a faint smile upon its lip
grotesque book, and quite without the iro
others of the Cautionary Tale genre — H
course, and even that Edwardian curio *Rut*
Heartless Homes.

It's an interesting fact that Helen Ba
about animals only, and about white childı
Squibba was another — were comparative failures. I wonder
why she usually chose to write about black children.

Dr. Bannerman: I think probably it was just she felt it made
it more interesting to a child, and I don't think black had any
unpleasant significance at that time. The Indians that we used
to meet were quite prepared to talk about black, without
feeling that there was anything derogatory in the word; I
think the derogatory idea crept in later.

Interviewer: Because now there's so much uneasiness isn't
there, that your mother's books are banned in the United
States?

Dr. Bannerman: United States they are banned, and I did
hear of some . . . out there where they've changed all the pictures of *Little Black Sambo* to make him a white child.

Interviewer: Little White Sambo.

Dr. Bannerman: I suppose they probably just call him Little
Sambo. I don't know why if they object to his being a little
black, because you'd never get a white child called Sambo.

Interviewer: No; well, it was a term of slightly patronising
endearment I suppose, like 'piccanniny', wasn't it, and yet
there is nothing of the slight feel of patronisation that you
get in some other old-fashioned children's books about coloured children, like Epaminondas, and one very strange Victorian
book called *The Story of the Naughty Little Coloured Coon,*
which I can quite see why people might object to.

Dr. Bannerman: No, I don't think she had any sort of colour
prejudice, and I think it was just to make it an interesting
story for children. Perhaps she felt that a black child was a
more romantic figure for a white child to read about.

Interviewer: I find that my children never even remark on

all, and this is the experience of nursery-school teachers.

Dr. Bannerman: I think it's the grown-ups who are affected by that. And there again, it's probably this business of writing for the child rather than the grown-ups.

Interviewer: Were you ever given any reason by the American publishers as to why . . .

Dr. Bannerman: Well, there was one cutting that we got which said that it was rather apt to inculcate racial and religious intolerance, but I've never understood why that should be. I suppose it was because black was considered a derogatory word, and as far as the religious thing went, the only thing I could think of is that his parents are called Black Jumbo and Black Mumbo, and that Mumbo-Jumbo is connected with religious intolerance, but otherwise I can see no connection with religion one way or the other.

Elizabeth Gard:

It seems absurd that an innocent production like Little Black Sambo should be fastidiously discarded—a ludicrously irrelevant gesture of apology for years of injustice. But *Little Black Sambo* will undoubtedly survive this muddled disapproval. He presides over the usual collection of by-products which surround popular children's classics. Dr. Bannerman remembers playing with toy figures of Sambo and the tiger. I remember sitting at a table-cloth with all the pictures blazoned round the edge. There have been cardboard cut-outs, gramophone records, and a Disney film, and now they're talking about nursery wallpaper. Little Black Sambo is big business.

(From *Books for Your Children*, Volume 5, Number 4, 1970.)

JANET HILL
Oh! Please Mr. Tiger

In March, 1972, Chatto and Windus, publishers of *Little Black Sambo* and other books by Helen Bannerman, drew renewed attention to them by advertising a boxed set containing all seven volumes, which their catalogue claimed "deserves a place on every child's bookshelf". Subsequently, Brian Alderson wrote an article "Banning Bannerman" in his column in *The Times* following a statement on the books he had elicited from the Central Committee of Teachers against Racism (TAR), which had roundly condemned them as books "which foster racist attitudes in children". They also said "In all of these books the underlying racist message is made all the more sinister by their appearance of innocence and charm", and claimed that "Along with the whimsical stories the reader swallows wholesale a totally patronizing attitude towards black people who are shown as greedy (Black Sambo eats 169 pancakes). . . .". The correspondence this article engendered in the columns of *The Times* was a predictable mixture of reasonable, hysterical and indignant letters.

I sympathize fully with the aims of TAR, but I regret the no doubt hasty statement they made on *Little Black Sambo,* which left them wide open to ridicule because of the terms in which they criticized this book, which has been surrounded by controversy, particularly in the United States, for many years. Seen in isolation, their comment that black people are shown as greedy because Sambo at the end of his adventures eats 169 pancakes is clearly laughable to anyone who knows the story, and deserves to be treated with ridicule. Equally the sentence about the "underlying racist message" and the implication that this is not only "sinister" but deliberate

191

shows a lamentable failure to acknowledge the historical context of the book. That TAR failed to take this factor into account is further shown by a comment in their letter to Brian Alderson, not quoted in his article, in which they claim that *"Little White Squibba* was clearly written as a conciliatory sop". This is to credit the author with low cunning as well as an awareness which would have made her thinking impossibly ahead of her time.

Helen Bannerman was born in Edinburgh, the daughter of an Army chaplain. When she was two, her family went to Madeira, where she stayed until the age of ten, when she was sent back to Scotland to be educated. In 1889 she married an Army doctor, and spent the next thirty years of her life in India. She wrote and illustrated *The Story of Little Black Sambo* for her two daughters in 1899, and it was published the same year. Another four titles had been published by 1909. *Sambo and the Twins* appeared in 1937, and *Little White Squibba* was published posthumously in 1966.

No one, least of all a librarian, could deny that her books are popular with children, and this is perfectly understandable. The stories have an engaging mixture of simplicity and absurdity which cannot fail to appeal, and show how well the author must have understood young children. There seems to be fairly general agreement that *Little Black Sambo* is by far the best of them, and it is the title mentioned in every reputable bibliography of children's books for the very young. Marcus Crouch in *Treasure Seekers and Borrowers* sums up succinctly:

> Throughout the history of children's literature, books have appeared which have had a success out of all proportion to their artistic merits. *Little Black Sambo,* crudely drawn, unpretentiously written, struck a chord to which children's hearts responded.

However, re-evaluation of books is a continual process. How do these books look in our multi-racial society in 1972? I believe this a valid question to ask, despite Brian Alderson's

comment in his article that "once external considerations are
allowed to affect our criteria for judging texts, critical anarchy supervenes. Billy Bunter is banned because there are fat
boys in Ipswich. . . ." To compare the attack on *Little Black
Sambo* with an attack on Billy Bunter is hardly justified. There
is no blatant prejudice against fat boys. They were not colon-
ized, taken into slavery or treated as inferior. White letter
writers to *The Times* wittily poured ridicule on the suggestion
that *Little Black Sambo* is racist, on the grounds that they had
never found it so, and some of them excelled at explaining
how delightfully tolerant they were. Other writers expressed
a different point of view:

As a black Briton, born and educated in this country, I
detested *Little Black Sambo* as much as I did the other textbooks which presented non-white people as living entirely
in primitive conditions and having no culture.

I asked black people in Lambeth for their views. A women's
group from a community association was extremely indignant, and found the books insulting to black people; they felt
that the names chosen were typical of those used by white
people to degrade black people; and that the stories were
totally outdated. The strength of their feelings matched those
of the writers to *The Times* who claimed that to dispense
with these books would be censorship. A teacher at a large
comprehensive school sent me a tape of a lively and good
humoured discussion recorded by a group of black teenagers.
They felt that everything about the books conveyed an image
of the black man living in mud huts, and that the way the
characters communicated with animals seemed to imply that
they were inferior, and close to the animal world.

Asked about the names, they said it wasn't just the names,
it was everything combined—the teeth and eyes, the "Al
Jolson" feeling, always smiling, "Yes Sir, No Sir"—the whole
idea of a smiling black, and the feeling that all you need to
do to make him happy is to put a bunch of mangoes in front
of him. . . . They made very perceptive comments about the

contrast between *Little Black Sambo* and *Little White Squibba*, by far the weakest of all the stories. They felt that in the latter book everything was so *nice*, and that it was noticeable that the animals were treated as pets. They also contrasted the first meeting of Squibba and Sambo with their respective tigers. When told by the tiger "I am going to eat you up", Squibba says "All right, try my sash". Sambo, faced by exactly the same situation, says "Oh! Please Mr Tiger, don't eat me up and I'll give you my beautiful little Red Coat" (always the picture of the docile nigger, they commented). Unlike most critics, they clearly saw the books in their historical context, and realized it was inevitable that a woman of Helen Bannerman's background and period would think and write as she did.

Marcus Crouch has called the illustrations "crudely drawn". They certainly are. *Little Black Sambo* as shown in full regalia on page 18 is a grinning stereotype with clownish eyes and huge mouth; the old woman on page 11 of *Little Black Quasha* turns round with a horrified face and her face is horrifying; Black Mumbo and Black Jumbo on page 82 of *Sambo and the Twins* jump for joy on hearing that the twins are safe, looking for all the world like a caricature of two cotton pickin' niggers in their gaily striped clothes. Admittedly the illustrations in *Little White Squibba* are excruciatingly badly drawn, but they are nice and dainty. To compare Squibba in her full finery on page 18 with the previously mentioned picture of Sambo is to point up the difference. She is unmistakably flesh and blood; a real human being with a dignity and poise befitting her station in life. He is an unreal caricature, less than human, with matchstick legs and golliwog face. Certainly, as the text claims, they both look grand. What is equally certain is that they inhabit different worlds.

Just as the illustrations are best discussed by contrasting *Little White Squibba* and the other books, so is the text. Not surprisingly the condescension of the writer is shown up most clearly by Squibba. She is sent books for her birthday "about little black children who had wonderful adventures in the

jungle", and wants to follow their example. Imitation may
be the sincerest form of flattery, but as the astute teenagers
who discussed the books pointed out, her experiences, although superficially the same as Sambo's, are in fact quite
different. She confronts each animal with aplomb, forestalls
every move, and calmly invites them all, including the tiger,
home to afternoon tea. They have pancakes, "because that
was what most of the little black children had had after their
adventures". Squibba is certainly secure in her tasteful and
well-ordered home, where even the pancakes have a delicacy
denied those served in the jungle. Meanwhile Sambo and his
friends live on in their strange quasi-African jungle home,
dancing around barefoot, surrounded by Indian tigers and
eating mangoes and pancakes.

Seen in this light I believe that the stories are condes-
cending and patronizing. I would not cite individual incidents
so much as the entire ambience of the books, particularly
as thrown into relief by *Little White Squibba.* The ambience
of a book is sometimes a difficult thing to pinpoint, as anyone
who has tried to prove that the ambience of so many English
children's books is comfortably middle-class will realize. I
freely admit that my own views about these books have
changed, and that I championed *Little Black Sambo* in print
some years ago, so that I can recognize that it is probably
difficult for those of us who are white and care about children's books to see them as other than charming little stories.
To call Helen Bannerman consciously racist is absurd. However, to recognize that her books are just another expression
of benevolent paternalism, the more insulting for its bene-
volence, is merely to show awareness of the deep roots of
racism in our history, culture and language. Her *outlook* is
certainly racist in the context of today.

Several letters to *The Times* pointed out gleefully that
young black children enjoy these stories, and quoted this is a
vindication of their racism. Sheila Ray makes the same point
in her book *Children's Fiction.* I find this patently absurd.
Four and five-year-olds, whether black or white, are not

generally noted for their perspicacity in identifying racism in books. However, black children gradually come to recognize how the white world sees them. A story told by Bernard Coard in a recent book (*How the West Indian Child is made Educationally Sub-Normal in the British School System*) should haunt us all. Appalled that a black child in his class always drew and painted himself white, the author offered to draw the child himself. When he drew him as he was, the boy was deeply upset and said that he had been made to look like a golliwog.

Helen Bannerman's books have had a long life, and the time has come to consign them to oblivion. They should have no place in a multi-racial society. What was it Marcus Crouch said? "Throughout the history of children's literature, books have appeared which have had a success out of all proportion to their artistic merits." They have had a fuss out of all proportion, too.

(From *The Times Literary Supplement*, November 3, 1972.)

PART FIVE
The Value of Children's Literature

INTRODUCTION

Most teachers and parents in general would agree that the reading of stories is a desirable thing with children. The days when public libraries used to ration fiction tickets in relation to non-fiction are over, and the condemnations once heard about the bad effects of novels on impressionable readers are now mostly reserved for certain television programmes. But I wonder how many adults, if pressed, could actively justify story-telling and reading, beyond negative reasons such as keeping children out of mischief or improving reading ability? If a more positive case for fiction is never realised, the whole children's literature movement can risk looking rather precious: an unnecessary fuss about a pleasant but otherwise trivial side of childhood.

Professor James Britton, in his introduction to *The Oxford Book of Stories for Juniors* (Teacher's Book), reprinted here, makes a good case for the importance of literature, linking reading with other verbal skills, and seeing it as an essential extension of any child's immediate experience. Yet one must also admit that there are certain children and adults, otherwise normal and well-adjusted individuals, who never read fiction and would be unhappy if required to do so. This is a point to a certain extent covered in the next short essay by Mary Warnock, *The Flight of the Imagination.* There are all sorts of effects and experiences *possible* from literature, but never any absolute guarantee that any one reader will arrive at any of these. When researchers have attempted to assess readers' reactions to particular books, the results have been very inconsistent. So although Professor Britton is surely right about the potential of fiction, we must never forget the different personality each reader brings to the book, sometimes making all the difference between an exciting literary experience and something that simply refuses to come alive. Why some perfectly literate individuals are uninterested in books is an interesting but at the moment unanswered question. But it is one that anyone interested in children's literature would do well to heed; trying to force books on to an able but reluctant reader can be a very short-sighted policy. Given that children have the right to read books for their own pleasure, we must also remember they have the right not to read them if they don't feel like it.

If we accept the power of fiction for those able to receive it, is the children's book a rather frail vessel in which to invest too much expectation? Do literary experiences really matter very much before maturity and access to adult literature? In another piece of writing, not included here, *Escape into childhood** Mary Warnock argues that the best children's books, although harmless in themselves, are straightforward forms of escape, necessarily lacking any real power of irony or artistic complexity. All right for children perhaps, but adults who persist in reading these limited, inevitably over-simplified works for their own sake are "metaphorically thumb-sucking", and shirking their intellectual responsibilities.

Perhaps there would be something odd about an adult who read nothing but children's books, and to this extent Mary Warnock's irritation with those university students who, she claims, show this sort of preference, would seem understandable (though I doubt whether this is a phenomenon that applies to more than a handful of undergraduates at a time, and even then as something of an affectation). Yet in this polemic, I think that Dr Warnock is led into some over-hasty remarks over the whole character of children's literature. Inevitably literature of this sort has to stop short at certain adult experience and modes of expression, but within the field that is left, there is still room for delicacy, irony and an appreciation of the complexity of things. There are limitations present in much writing for adults too, self-imposed

* *New Society,* May 13, 1971.

by the climate of 20th century fiction. As Jill Paton Walsh points out in the last article, *The Rainbow Surface,* certain ways of writing beyond the tradition of the realistic, contemporary novel are no longer so acceptable to the adult market; would Dickens, let alone Homer, be writing for children if he were alive today? Yet who could say that adults, as well as children, have no need of this sort of writing? In this sense, it is surely quite permissable for the adult to dip into the so-called children's market, especially now that it has extended to include a whole range of literature enjoyed by adults in former times with no sense of literary slumming at all. Miss Paton Walsh is herself a writer for both children and adults; her latest book, *The Emperor's Winding Sheet,** is set at the end of the Byzantine Empire, and won the Whitbread award for children's fiction for 1974.

* Macmillan, 1974.

JAMES BRITTON
from *The Oxford Book of Stories for Juniors—Introduction*

I think the first thing to notice is that stories and poems will have more in common with children's speaking and writing than will any other forms of the written language in use in school. Their language, in speech or writing, and the language of poems and stories are in the main forms of what I would call 'personal language'. It is as much as most children can do to see the world, and describe it, from their own individual points of view. They may begin to be able to see things from some other person's point of view—their mother's or their sister's—but that is still a long way from seeing things in general from the point of view of people in general. The *impersonal* viewpoint—that common to anybody or every-body—is arrived at by shedding those elements in our experience that are peculiar to ourselves, not common to all observers, or peculiar to one occurrence, not common to all repetitions of an occurrence. The impersonal view is arrived at therefore by a process of elimination: and this takes time and is something that has to be learnt. (It is a stage in mental development rather akin to the stage in language development where the word can first be used in place of the thing.)

I suggest that poems and stories differ from other forms of writing met in school in precisely this way. The poet or the story-writer is concerned in the first place to put into his work what pleases him. The principle on which he selects and arranges his material is, in the long run, that of pleasing himself. The historian, the scientist, the text-book writer—like the newspaper reporter—must meet other demands and is not free simply to please himself. To make of the raw material of experience a design that pleases oneself is, in fact, to present a purely personal viewpoint. A child's use of language is of necessity personal: the poet and the story-teller use a personal language from choice.

The subjects that make up the school curriculum represent areas of common concern and common knowledge for people living in our society. The experiences in which one child differs most from another, therefore, are excluded from this curriculum—necessarily and by design. But it is these individual and personal things that poets and story-tellers deal with: home life, relations with mothers and fathers and brothers and sisters, events that are important because of the emotions involved—exciting adventures, life-and-death struggles, heroic and tragic and heart-warming incidents.

There is surely no need to question whether such matters deserve a place in school work: they are as much an extension of a child's accumulated experience (and therefore his capacity to make something of fresh experience) as are the matters of common knowledge and social concern, the truths of history and geography and science.

But I would take the argument further: a child approaches the facts of history by involving himself in a personal way with the lives of people of past ages. It is through exciting adventures, life-and-death struggles, heroic and tragic and heart-warming incidents that he moves towards an impersonal appreciation of the external facts. At an early stage then there will be little difference between the stories about other times that lead out to the truths of history—or the stories about other countries that lead out to the truths of geography—and the stories about fathers and mothers and giants and witches and dogs and cats, the stories that lead to more stories and remain for a life-time a means of extending our experience by identifying ourselves with the personal lives of such people as Huckleberry Finn and Tom Jones and Moll Flanders and Anna Karenina and King Lear—to mention the first that come to mind.

Here I think we can begin to make a rough distinction

between poems and stories. Poetry is the most personal, the most individual, kind of writing. A poem speaks to us intimately or not at all: it has little direct relation with the practical routines of our everyday lives. What poetry does above all, I believe, is to mediate experience for us, help us to resolve conflicts and come to terms with intractable events.

But I must add here that stories about witches and giants seem to me very like poetry in this respect. Children like writing them for reasons they cannot understand—because they are able in using symbols to handle problems which they could not state and cannot therefore handle directly. How often, for example, the witch in a child's story speaks with the voice of a scolding mother! Again, can we doubt that the six-year-old writer of the following was dealing with her own plight in the only terms available to her?

There was a child of a witch, who was ugly, he had pointed ears thin legs and was born in a cave, he flew in the air holding on nothing just playing games.

When he saw ordinary girls and boys he hit them with his broom stick. A cat came along, he arched his back at the girls and boys and made them run away. When they had gone far away the cat meeowed softly at the witch child, the cat loved the child, the child loved the cat the cat was the onlee thing the child loved in the world.

The first book in this series contains a good many stories of this kind, stories in which, whether they read them or write them, children are coming to terms with experience. I believe they need them at this stage because, being very active and yet very inexperienced explorers and interpreters of the world they live in, they receive conflicting impressions as to its nature. We construct a picture of the world as it *is* or as it *seems* to us; at this stage of inexperience there is more 'seems' in the picture than 'is', and the picture requires, therefore, constant adjustment in the light of fresh experience. Whether my explanation is the right one or not, it does appear that most children at this age enter into and enjoy myths and folk tales and legends.

By the time the third book in the series is reached the emphasis has changed. The need for fantasy continues (and will do, of course, throughout life) but takes second place, for most children, to a growing curiosity about the real world and so an interest in stories of other people's lives. Perhaps there is henceforward a rough differentiation of function: poems continue to help us to come to terms with experience, stories provide an extension of our experience into the lives of others. This would explain the fact that we certainly tend to treat them differently in school.

The underlying difference is one I have already suggested: stories are more directly related to our ordinary everyday lives and so more readily extended, in a thousand-and-one directions, away from the story into the active concerns of everyday life. Talk in the classroom about a story that has just been read will have two purposes therefore. Moving between the story and the individual lives of the children it will help them to make the story their own, see it in terms of their own lives: much of this talk will be highly individual and personal. But talk will also move out from the story in directions suggested by the children's curiosity: things mentioned in the story may further existing interests or stimulate fresh ones: the move will be out towards things to do, to find out, to think and talk and write about. Here then is one bridge between a child's personal starting point and the impersonal facts of our existence. . . .

Mastery of impersonal language is the gateway to all further education, whether in school, college, university, or out. But impersonal language can only safely and effectively be handled by those who can give it personal meaning. Hence the danger of moving prematurely into the textbook language of facts and general statements, and the importance of giving full scope for the development of each individual child's personal experience and interest and knowledge. An involvement in other men's lives is the first step away from the limitations of the individual child's-eye view, and stories, as chapters in other men's lives, real or imaginary, have therefore at this stage an indispensable role to play.

(From the 'Introduction' to *The Oxford Book of Stories for Juniors,* Teacher's Book, 1965.)

MARY WARNOCK
The Flight of the Imagination

The most lasting and radical effect of a university education, particularly in history, philosophy or natural sciences, seems to be an overwhelming caution in answering certain questions; a caution which arises from respect for the notion of *evidence*. Social scientists and psychologists do not appear to suffer from this caution in quite the same way.

One such question, which many people raise, and sceptics are not prepared to answer, is concerned with the permanent effect on people of what they read. Plato, Aristotle and others have been happy to state dogmatically what are the effects, for good or ill, of literature on readers, or plays on viewers. But the more one thinks of the problem, in a less exalted context than the *Republic* or the *Poetics,* the less possible it is to see how one could possibly collect evidence to show that, for example, a particular kind of children's book had a particular effect on its readers. One might show that certain books were, by objective standards, ill-written, or that they contained an objectionable moral, or even that some books frightened their readers. But what one could not show would be the long-term effect on children of having been frightened, or exposed to illiterate stories.

It is certain that some books bore children; and it would, in principle, be possible to find out which. But it would not be possible in the same way to determine the long-term effect on them of boredom. Even in such apparently straightforward cases as that of the frightening or non-frightening in literature, one is likely fairly soon to come up against theories rather than facts: and such facts as there are do not seem to be enough to form the basis of any prediction.

My own childhood horrors in books were, first, a now long-forgotten work called *The Adventures of Mabel,* of which I can remember nothing except one terrible picture, and a dreadful, sinister atmosphere; and, secondly, the picture of the inside of the railway carriage in *Alice Through the Looking-Glass.* One of my children was likewise terrified of this picture, but the others were not. My youngest child was utterly terrified of a picture of a large cup, in a most harmless and agreeable book called *The Adventures of Ant and Bee,* which many children must have read with profit and pleasure. So, even at this level, it is hard to isolate the frightening, or separate the safe from the dangerous—assuming we knew that being frightened *was dangerous,* which it probably is not.

But despite the lack of facts, theories obviously abound. One frequently hears of librarians in public libraries refusing to keep this children's book or that. And, worse than that, it is clear that authors of children's books themselves often operate on some theory of the imagination which is never made explicit, but the existence of which one can deduce from the nature of their work. For example, there is a large United Nations category of children's books which have in common the laudable aim of awakening children to the existence of countries other than their own (especially developing countries), and making them interest themselves in problems and ways of life different from any that they have personally experienced. The theory here seems to be that the imagination needs to be stretched, or exercised; and that once the reader has an imaginative grasp of the new material, he will retain a sympathy with the kind of people with whom he identified himself in the plot.

This theory is by no means new, though probably the children's books about foreign parts are very much more numerous than they used to be. I remember the feeling of despair which I experienced when told by a teacher at school that it was *always* better to read books about distant lands than about England, and *always* better to read about people as little like oneself as possible. A terrible vista of novels about

208

middle-aged men in China rose up before me, and, with it, the sinking premonition of boredom.

The question to which it is essential to know the answer is simply whether there is any force in this kind of theory. Is the imagination like a muscle which, if it is not exercised, will atrophy? And if the imagination is given more to do in reading about alien forms of life—an assumption in itself open to doubt—does this energetic use of the faculty in one sphere carry over to be applied in real life, or does it not?

At a commonsense level, one feels inclined to say that the most effective books, in the sense of the books which become most completely part of one's imaginative life, must at the very least also be the most memorable. And one great defect that the United Nations class of books has is the total non-memorability of the names of the child-heroes. (That this is not a fatal bar for grown-ups is shown by the powerful effect of novelists like Solzhenitsyn; and it is not therefore *necessarily* fatal for children either, but it creates an extra obstacle.)

Then again, it seems almost a law that one's imagination operates most powerfully in areas which could conceivably be real for one. Thus, at a low level, many of the most fanatical readers of pony books are those who do not possess ponies, but feel that, if things were a little different, they might. If one is interested in birds, it may be, in some impersonal way, nice to read about exotic birds in South America, but it is far more exciting to read about birds which are—however rarely—to be seen in England, if that is where one lives. There is a completely different kind of fascination surrounding the bittern or the great northern diver or the chough.

It may be objected that this law, if it is one, should not be allowed to dominate the literary imagination. If it were, then all literature would be enjoyed only if it fitted in with the reader's fantasy life, and writing novels would be as much a matter of calculating the fantasies of the public as writing advertising copy is. The teacher at school who urged us to read about foreign parts was not just trying to stop us reading school stories, but also trying to inculcate a principle—to help us rise above *Woman's Own,* Ian Fleming and Iris Murdoch.

There is much truth in this principle. However, the fact that some novels do fit in with our fantasies does not necessarily entail that they were specially created to do so, nor that they are therefore disreputable. And some novels have such independent power over our imagination that they may create a wholly new fantasy for us. The romantic conception of the railway in Russia is an entirely factitious fantasy, created originally by the greatness of Russian novelists.

Moreover, there are two points here which should not be confused. One is the probably legitimate point that we ought not to indulge our fantasies in reading, or ought not to do *only* this. The second is the more dubious suggestion that we can do positive good to ourselves by reading about things beyond our experience or even our dreams.

It should not be thought that only so will our imaginations be at work. There is a kind of imagination which we bring into play when we read autobiography, which has nothing to do with remoteness or exoticism. There is an extraordinary pleasure to be found in the directness with which we can enter somebody else's life, and feel what they felt, and see things with their eyes. If more people kept and published diaries, we should have more of this imaginative pleasure at our disposal.

A diary should be frequently exclamatory in tone, and not too self-consciously reflective. We should be allowed to see the cases—as we can in the passages of Simone de Beauvoir's diary, which form part of her autobiography—where the author has to exhort himself, when he is overcome, or simply stuck for words. It is infinitely more effective, from the reader's point of view, to overhear the diarist say, "Tomorrow I *must* begin to work, I really *will,*" than to be told, as part of a narrative, "I resolved to start work the next day." We should be allowed to witness the author's first impressions of places or people with whom later he becomes familiar and about whom he perhaps radically changes his views. We should be allowed to see him starting hopefully on some project which later turns out to be a mistake or a bore.

The best autobiography aspires to the condition of a diary. It is extraordinary how little difference it makes whether we feel that we like or dislike the author. Somehow, if the imaginative exercise succeeds, the question ceases to arise. We ask it no more than we seriously ask if we like or dislike ourselves, or our children. This kind of identification with another person is undoubtedly the result of the exercise of the imagination.

Perhaps the real question is whether, apart from the immediate pleasures of the imagination, there is any permanent effect in us of *having* exercised our imagination in a particular way. This is the question to which the theorists, including librarians and authors of children's books, seem to think that there is an answer, and to which the academic sceptics tend to believe that, if there is, we could never know it.

(From *New Society,* August 6, 1970.)

JILL PATON WALSH
The Rainbow Surface

Is there such a thing as a children's book? Is the children's book an art form, distinct from other fiction, having its own particular excellence? Or is it just the novel made easy, in which everything is the same as in an adult book, only less so? If the second possibility were the truth it would surely be the case that all (rather than some, as Kevin Crossley-Holland recently suggested) children's authors would know themselves for adult authors manqué. If children's books are themselves an art form, albeit a minor art, then a writer may perfectly well have a talent more apt to them than to mainstream fiction, just as he may have a talent more apt to short stories than to novels.

From the writer's standpoint, there certainly is such a thing as a children's book, because a number of more or less conscious adjustments have to be made in writing them. The children's book presents a technically most difficult, technically most interesting problem—that of making a fully serious adult statement, as a good novel of any kind does, and making it utterly simple and transparent. It seems to me to be a dereliction of some kind, almost a betrayal of the young reader, to get out of the difficulty by putting down the adult's burden of knowledge, and experience, and speaking childishly; but the need for comprehensibility imposes an emotional obliqueness, an indirectness of approach, which like elision and partial statement in poetry is often itself a source of aesthetic power. I imagine the perfectly achieved children's book something like a soap-bubble; all you can see is a surface—a lovely rainbow thing to attract the youngest on-looker—but the whole is shaped and sustained by the pressure of adult emotion, present but invisible, like the air within the bubble. Many themes can be treated indirectly in this way which crudely and directly broached would not be "suitable" for children; perhaps one may hope their emotions may be educated by the shape of the rainbow surface, in preparation for more conscious understanding of hard things. I am thinking here of a book like *The Owl Service.*

The simplicity-significance problem is, however, a profoundly complex one, to which there is more than one solution. In another kind of book the adult statement runs alongside, rather than within, the book; a sort of exterior analogue. Here I have in mind *The Mouse and his Child,* a book which no adult could read without seeing in it a fable of our times, our century familiar with rubble heaps, with destruction, with displaced persons. But the child with his merciful short memory reads an unhaunted tale, a tale for its own sake, complete and satisfying for itself. Indeed, in this case, he may even be *protected* to some degree by the make-believe quality inherent in humanized toys, small mammals, etc. as characters, from the realization of the truth that people too have been battered, discarded, exploited and hounded like that. Read in innocence, the book is a lesson in the long and necessarily painful education of the heart.

Another type of solution is the use of fantasy or surrealism (dreams, magic, time shifts, et al.) to make Freudian journeys to the heart of the interior. This is not the kind of book I write, yet from my writer's viewpoint it seems clear that this approach offers a whole range of interesting and fruitful solutions to the significance-simplicity problem, at the cost of extreme difficulties in execution. Penelope Farmer once pointed out to me that even the simplest magical occurrence, if met in real life, would in fact terrify to the point of unhinging minds; she is right, and this generates a continuous credibility problem about such stories, demanding a high degree of literary skill to make them seem real. For no child will tremble for the danger threatening a Hobbit, if he does not believe in Hobbits. Likewise in stories which use dream there is an ever-present technical difficulty; dreams "float", and it is difficult to use them in an advancing narrative structure. Nevertheless, some of the most beautiful and powerful children's books are of this kind, when the writer measures up to the task—Catherine Storr's *Marianne Dreams,* for example, or William Mayne's recent *A Game of Dark.*

In this book the "plot", with danger, the need for courage, the narrative tension, has been transposed to the surreal level, so that the reality of Donald's life appears as interruptions in the dream, rather than the dream interrupting reality. Adult understanding of this book demands comprehension of the relation of life and dream; but the transposing device ensures that the least aware reader following the "story" will have his attention nailed at the level of nightmare. This book is as terrifying as self-knowledge, which is saying a lot. I do not doubt, however, that terror is good for children. I am in favour of exercising all the muscles of the heart. It is a device with story that brings off this tour de force. The story is indispensable to children's books—the necessary continuous thread to bring young readers through any kind of labyrinth. The children's book is an essentially narrative form, being in this respect much less versatile than the mainstream novel, which can do other things as well, or instead.

Let us look now at the current relationship between adult fiction and children's books. I think there is no doubt it is a very curious one. I am not the first person to be dazzled by the galaxy of formidable talents that adorn contemporary children's literature. In any other age most of them would have been let out of the nursery, and allowed to entertain the adults. Their talents would have been appropriate to the novel, when obliquity and indirectness were compulsory in the treatment of a vast swathe of adult experience. That restraint has now completely gone; it may well be that some contemporary writers are voluntarily seeking a stimulating discipline in choosing to write for children. But we all work in a context; and the present context is one in which *any* book with a strong plot and no extreme erotic scenes, and *any* book dealing in magic or fantasy seems to many people to be a book for children.

The *Odyssey* has for 3,000-odd years attracted the serious attention of the most brilliant and educated minds, yet if it were written today there is no doubt it would be published for children. One can almost imagine the reviews: "Mr Homer has a lively vein of invention and a fresh eye for detail that will entrance the nine to ten-year-old . . ." and then a disapproving eyebrow raised at the slaughter of the suitors. In this context it is not surprising that there is an upsurge of interest in children's books; much of it is not pedagogic, or parental at all, but is the simple pleasure of a reader enjoying himself. Really it seems to me that the defining quality of children's literature is to be sought not in children, nor in children's writers, but in the peculiarities of the adult market.

The mainstream novel in our century has turned its back on the story—and the space, and hopefulness, that good stories need: the epic balance, that to "they wept long and bitterly for their comrades" always adds, "and then prepared a meal and slept till morning" has come to be felt by the adult sensibility as unreal, deluding, wishful thinking. But the appetite for story remains. It has lived in humble forms before, when the grander literature disowned it. It has lived in ballad and broadsheet, and unwritten folk tale. For a while in the nineteenth century the novel in all its splendour served it, and now it runs in byways again, in spy-thrillers, and science fiction, and children's books.

Children's writers will probably always meet with a good deal of condescension; some of it from people whose inability to see the multivalency of a good children's book hardly inspires confidence in their ability to read the kind of difficult modern novel that the children's writer does not write; we should blow our soap bubbles unconcerned; we are working in a literary tradition that goes back not to *Ulysses* but to Odysseus.

(From *The Times Literary Supplement,* December 3, 1971.)

SELECT BIBLIOGRAPHY

Introduction

Darton, F.J.H., *Children's Books in England: Five Centuries of Social Life* (second edition, Cambridge, University Press, 1958).

Egoff, S. (ed.), *Only Connect: Readings on Children's Literature* (Oxford, University Press, 1969).

Fisher, M., *Intent upon Reading* (second edition, London, Brockhampton, 1964).

Muir, P., *English Children's Books, 1600-1900* (second edition, London, Batsford; New York, Praeger, 1969).

Townsend, J.R., *A Sense of Story: Essays on Contemporary Writers for Children* (London, Longman; New York, Lippincott, 1971).

Townsend, J.R., *Written for Children*, (Harmondsworth, Penguin Kestrel Books; New York, Lothrop, revised edition 1974).

Trease, G., *Tales out of School* (London, Heinemann; New York, Dufour, 1964).

Fairy Stories

Briggs, K.M., *The Fairies in English Tradition and Literature* (London, Routledge; Chicago, University Press ,1967).

Chukovsky, K., *From Two to Five* (California, University Press, 1966).

Cook, E., *The Ordinary and the Fabulous* (Cambridge, University Press, 1969).

Duffy, M., *The Erotic World of Faery* (London, Hodder, 1972).

217

Michaelis — Jena, R., *The Brothers Grimm* (London, Routledge, New York, Praeger, 1970).

Opie, I. and P., *The Classic Fairy Tales* (Oxford, University Press, 1974).

Tolkien, J.R.R., *Tree and Leaf* (London, Allen and Unwin; New York, Houghton Mifflin, 1964).

Comics

Alderson, C., *Magazines Teenagers Read* (Oxford, Pergamon, 1968).

Feiffer, J., *The Great Comic Book Heroes* (Harmondsworth, Allen Lane, The Penguin Press, 1967).

Perry, G., *The Penguin Book of Comics* (Harmondsworth, Allen Lane, The Penguin Press, 1971).

Turner, E.S., *Boys will be Boys* (London, Michael Joseph; New York, Finch Press, New edition 1975).

Wertham, F., *Seduction of the Innocent* (London, Museum Press, New York, Kennikat Press, 1955).

Children's Books and Fear

de la Mare, W., *Early One Morning in the Spring: Chapters on Children and on Childhood* (London, Faber, 1935).

Lewis, C.S., *Surprised by Joy* (London, Bles; New York, Harcourt, Brace, Jovanovich, 1955).

Morpurgo, J.E. (ed), *The Autobiography of Leigh Hunt,* (London, The Cresset Press; New York, Dufour, 1948).

Pickard, P.M., *I Could a Tale Unfold* (London, Tavistock, 1961).

Children's Classics and Some Controversies

Green, P., *Kenneth Grahame* (London, Murray, 1959).

Hurlimann, B., *Three Centuries of Children's Books in Europe* (see chapter on 'Barbar') (Oxford, University Press, 1967).

Kocher, P., *Master of Middle Earth: The Achievement of J.R.R. Tolkien* (London, Thames and Hudson; New York,

Houghton Mifflin, 1973).

Lane, M., *The Tale of Beatrix Potter* (second edition, London, Warne, 1968).

The Value of Children's Literature

Cameron, E., *The Green and Burning Tree* (Boston, Little Brown, 1969).

Chambers, A., *Introducing Books to Children* (London, Heinemann, 1973).

D'Arcy, P., *Reading for Meaning: Volume 2. The Reader's Response* (London, Hutchinson, 1973).

Haviland, V. (ed.)., *Children and Literature: Views and Reviews* (New York; Scott, Foreman and Co., 1973; London, Bodley Head, 1974).

Hazard, P., *Books, Children and Men* (Boston, Horn Books, 1944).

Hildick, W., *Children and Fiction* (London, Evans; New York, World Publishing Co., 1970).

INDEX